Born Ready!
An Actor's Handbook

# BORN READY!

## AN ACTOR'S HANDBOOK

CAIRN A. MOORE

J. GORDON SHILLINGFORD
PUBLISHING INC

*Born Ready! An Actor's Handbook*
first published 2025 by J. Gordon Shillingford Publishing Inc.


Editor: Glenda MacFarlane
Cover design by Doowah Design
Cover photo of Cairn A. Moore by Kevin McIntyre Photography



Printed and bound in Canada on 100% post-consumer recycled paper.

We acknowledge the financial support of the Canada Council for the Arts, the Government of Canada, the Manitoba Arts Council and the Government of Manitoba for our publishing program.

Canada Council for the Arts | Conseil des arts du Canada | Funded by the Government of Canada | Canada | Manitoba Arts Council | Conseil des arts du Manitoba | Manitoba

*Library and Archives Canada Cataloguing in Publication*

Title: Born ready! : an actor's handbook / Cairn A. Moore.
Names: Moore, Cairn A., 1963- author
Identifiers: Canadiana 20250267063 | ISBN 9781990738715 (softcover)
Subjects: LCSH: Acting—Vocational guidance—Handbooks, manuals, etc. | LCSH: Acting—Handbooks, manuals, etc. | LCSH: Acting—Auditions—Handbooks, manuals, etc. | LCSH: Acting—Psychological aspects. | LCGFT: Handbooks and manuals.
Classification: LCC PN2055 .M66 2025 | DDC 792.02/8023—dc23

J. Gordon Shillingford Publishing
P.O. Box 86, RPO Corydon Avenue, Winnipeg, MB Canada R3M 3S3

*Dedicated to all my beautiful caterpillars*

## CONTENTS

# FOREWORD

The beauty of acting is how it allows us to become more human and more humane. Embodying another person's lived experience changes us, whether we plan to be professional actors or not. I've seen numerous acting students go on to incredible careers in an array of disciplines. Their success is due to the self-awareness, confidence, empathy, and analytical skills that come from the craft of acting. In my current teaching through Walls to Bridges in carceral settings, I see firsthand the transformational potential of theatre. So, picking up this book and choosing to explore the topic is a wonderful step in personal and/or professional development.

In addition, you are embarking on a journey guided adeptly by an artist and human who is greatly respected in the theatre community. I've had the honour of knowing Cairn Moore since my early time arriving in Winnipeg (via Toronto.) Although I grew up in Saskatoon, my studies and early work took me all over the country and even abroad. Winnipeg was promoted to me as the perfect middle, not too big or too small and with a vibrant arts sector. Cairn was teaching at the Prairie Theatre Exchange School when I arrived and our paths first crossed. It soon became clear that she embodied the notion of community that was one of Winnipeg's selling points. I went on to work with Cairn as an actor, playwright and collaborator. We had the privilege of working with criminalized women and co-writing the play *Jail Baby*, then gathering stories around mental health for *Breaking Through*. Cairn's past work in community allowed her to facilitate workshops with a range of participants and allow them to see the power of theatre.

We are now colleagues at the University of Winnipeg, dedicated to teaching the next generation of theatre artists. I have seen firsthand the value of Cairn's work with students of all ages and backgrounds. Students love working with her! She truly builds community in her classroom and that is a gift, especially at a time of divisiveness and isolation. In her lengthy teaching career, she has supported hundreds of emerging actors and those who love acting. Now with Actors Studio, which she owns and operates, she has been able to train an even wider range of artists.

I have been teaching acting for twenty-five years, from beginners to senior students. I can attest to the fact that there are no shortcuts to being an engaging performer nor quick ways to shine on stage. It is a process, a lot of hard work, and commitment. The first step is often just becoming conscious of what it is you do not know and understanding the fundamentals. This book is a great resource to do just that. Then working on technique and developing your own craft will be a life-long process for those who want to continue.

Although I don't believe there is one single acting technique that works for all actors or styles of theatre, there are key concepts that will allow for growth. This book provides many tools regularly used in introductory theatre and acting courses, providing the reader with a foundational knowledge and methods to test out as they find what will be most valuable in their own toolbox. Key concepts from the need for bravery to respecting the playwright's punctuation, make the book valuable for all those interested in the art of performance. Plus, it is written in Cairn's own wonderful voice, so rife with personality!

*Hope McIntyre, Associate Professor, University of Winnipeg*

# PROLOGUE

## A Few Words Before We Begin

Although I teach theatre at the university level, this book is designed to be a very practical guide for actors, whether they are in an academic setting or not. My teaching experience is multi-faceted. I have taught students of every age, from every walk of life, in every scenario imaginable: university, professional theatres, social services, rural communities, reserves throughout Manitoba, senior care homes, large and small businesses, federal and provincial prisons, mental health facilities, and, most recently, my own theatre school, Actors Studio with Cairn Moore.

Eclectic resume aside, my many years of teaching first-year performance at the University of Winnipeg in Friendly Manitoba have led me to this book, which, by the way, I have been threatening to write forever—and with good reason. First, there is a desperate need for a simply stated guidebook for developing actors that doesn't weigh fifty pounds and isn't a complete yawner to read. Not long ago, my students' Intro to Performance reading list included a dated guidebook I used in my first year of studies a million years ago. Okay, maybe not quite a million, but you get the idea. Over the years, I have sought out and experimented with countless alternatives, but they fell short…so now, after twenty-five long years of complaining, I have—drumroll, please—decided to write the damn book myself!

And why not? My students have been badgering me to spill my theatre tea for as long as I can remember, and upon reflection, I realized I had quite a bit of tea to spill. But I wanted to do the spilling in a particular way. There are a whole lot of acting books out there, and if I were going to add yet another, mine needed to offer something different.

For starters, it needed to be inclusive. Acting, after all, is for everyone. No fancy words to look up, just a conversational handbook that is fresh and inspirational, whether the reader has been taking acting classes since childhood or is coming on board in the final chapter of their life.

No matter what brings you to acting at this point in your life, it is never too late! A few years ago I had this spunky, sharp, creative woman in her late eighties who signed on for a seniors' acting class so she could write and perform her own eulogy! Her purpose? She wanted to leave it for her family to watch upon her passing. And so she did. Every one of you is unique, with boundless creative potential. My job within these pages is merely to open a door and guide you through it. To offer you some strategies. Mostly to help you get out of your own way.

Second, said book would not only need to cover acting essentials such as scene analysis and acting theory, but would also need to look to the future. And the future is bright! There has never been a better time to be an actor. Increasingly, university and conservatory acting programs are adopting safe rehearsal practices and are training actors in ways that protect their mental health.

I also wanted to give you the lowdown on theatre etiquette. Yes, you heard right. I will share all of the lessons I learned as a developing actor that I wish someone had shared with me but didn't. This will save you a great deal of time and embarrassment because, unlike me, you will not be forced to learn them the hard way.

Above all else, I wanted this book to address an alarming trend: Every year, more and more students arrive on my doorstep overcome with anxiety and self-doubt. Not the kind of nervousness one would expect from a student beginning a new class in a room full of strangers, either. This is the kind of anxiety that shuts you down and paralyzes you. The kind of fear that has my students running to the bathroom (what I've heard a few of them refer to as "bathroom camping") to have a panic attack. No one should have to feel like that! Which is why I am going to offer you some strategies to help you stay in the room, like taking gentle care of your artist self, learning how to celebrate failure and how to build and maintain confidence.

My goal here was to write the kind of acting handbook I wish was available to me on my journey as a developing actor—*Born Ready!* is that book. But before we dive in, I have one very important question to ask…

## Are You Born Ready?

Whether my university students arrive in the studio with no experience or truckloads of it, they all have one thing in common—anxiety. Even that person in class who seems like they have their act together has moments of anxiety and self-doubt. And that's okay; anxiety is a normal emotion we all experience. To feel anxious is to be human. It's when it affects our daily lives that it becomes an issue. And it is definitely affecting our daily lives. Everywhere I go, young people are talking about anxiety. Unfortunately, talking about it isn't going to make it go away. We need to act. How can you do your best acting (or your best anything) when the anxiety monster is calling the shots?

Long ago, I realized that 80% of my time is spent convincing students to believe in themselves and the other 20% teaching them the skills they need to do that. Recently, I made a discovery that affected not only me in a profound way: ***Saying is believing.*** I read somewhere that if you are having a crappy day but force yourself to smile despite it, you will not only feel happier, but you will also spread a little sunshine. It turns out that smiling is contagious! When I read this, I was skeptical, but I decided to give it a whirl. Guess what? It works!

I'm not going to lie; not every person will return your smile, but most will. More importantly, the simple act of slapping a smile on your face will instantly lift your spirits. Now, this isn't a novel idea; psychologists have been preaching it for decades, but it got me thinking…maybe there is something to this whole "fake it till you make it" philosophy.

And so the experiment began, with my students as my unwitting lab rats. Before presenting their scene or monologue, I would ask, "Are you ready?" Most of the time, they would respond with a low-energy "Yah" or "I guess" or give me a handful of excuses about having zero time to rehearse, putting them in a negative head space before they even opened their mouths. Note to self: Never start your scene or monologue with an apology!

That's when I told them that no matter how they were feeling at that moment, or whether they believed the words coming out of their mouths, they needed to reply to the question "Are you ready?" with a very enthusiastic "Born Ready!!!" If they gave me 50% enthusiasm instead of 100%, I made them say it again. And again. I'm pretty sure some of them wanted to punch me in the face. Still, I persisted. The result was mind-blowing! Just saying those two words out loud instantly boosted their confidence. They were 50% there. And the icing on the cake? The more often they said it, the closer they came to believing it. I was definitely on to something!

I have to confess that in some cases, *not saying is believing.* For instance, I had a fantastic student with incredible talent who constantly apologized for her work—out loud—after everything she did. The only thing getting in the way of this young woman's success was her! So, I banned her from apologizing. At first, it drove her mad. The habit of apologizing was so deeply ingrained in her that it took an entire university year to get her to stop. Once she did, it was like watching a caterpillar become a butterfly.

Be a butterfly. Give yourself a break! From this moment forward, you are *Born Ready!* Again, I don't care if you believe what you are saying because I know that, in time, you will start to believe. Nothing is going to change overnight. It took a long time to develop the "talk-smack-about-yourself" habit, so it's going to take a long time to break it.

So, before we embark on this incredible, life-changing, creative journey together, answer me this: Are you Born Ready? I'm not playing here. I want commitment! I want you to sign on the dotted line. Go on. I'm waiting…I'm still waiting…

If you are Born Ready (or you're not but are willing to say you are), sign below.

I, ____________________ ____________________, declare myself "Born Ready."

______________________________________________

*(Your signature)*

Congratulations! You are officially halfway to believing! Turn the page, and let's start working on the other half!

# ACT I: THEATRE ETIQUETTE

## Heed the Rules of the Road

If you are going to take the written part of your driver's test, you aren't going to show up at the test site before studying the rules of the road, right? Just like knowing the rules of the road is critical to passing your driver's test, being versed in theatre etiquette is the key to surviving and thriving in the theatre world, which brings me to my next point…

## Don't Be a Jerk!

This is the most useful theatre etiquette tip I can give you. I don't care how talented you are, if you get a reputation for being a jerk it is nearly impossible to overcome. Which is why, in this chapter I will share with you the most common jerk behaviours to avoid.

**The Bottom Line:**

DON'T BE A JERK!

## Follow the Golden Rule

The golden rule is a universal code of conduct familiar to most of us. It's pretty basic: Treat others like you would want them to treat you. Makes sense. The incentive for practising this rule is knowing that when you do, you will contribute to a professional work environment. The people you work and interact with will take note of your professionalism or lack thereof. Besides, who doesn't like a little harmony in the workplace? It's a win-win. Respect and work ethic are incredibly important, whether in an acting class or rehearsing for a show.

The rehearsal hall is a sacred place, a sandbox in which to play without distraction. When actors are inconsiderate, it tells everyone else in the room that they don't care about anyone's work but their own. This affects the team as a whole and diminishes the quality of the work. It will also affect your chances of working with those people again.

**The Bottom Line:**

> If you treat others respectfully and kindly, you will get the same in return. (Most of the time.)

## Nurture Your Artist Connections

One of my closest colleagues, Hope McIntyre, taught me the importance of nurturing friendships in the theatre community. She didn't teach by telling; she taught by doing. Following in her footsteps, I quickly learned that theatre folks help each other out all the time.

If I need a couple of costume pieces and have trouble finding them, I pick up the phone. If I have a film audition and I need someone to do off-lines, I have only to ask. After I have written a scene, and I need to hear it out loud, I call on my WWF friends (Women Writing Furiously), and they come to the rescue. If I have an idea for a play, I bounce it off my theatre friends. While writing this book, I called on actors, novelists, professors, students and friends to read over parts of the book and provide me with honest feedback. They all said yes! They all gave generously of themselves because they know I would do the same for any of them. Theatre karma—you get what you give.

## Avoid Bad-Mouthing Other People

*"Bad-mouthing someone only reveals your own character, not theirs."—Unknown*

A classic jerk move is to bad-mouth other people in the theatre community. In another section of this book, I talk about the importance of not bad-mouthing yourself, but it is just as important not to talk negatively about other people (unless you are reporting inappropriate or abusive behaviour).

Theatre communities are pretty tight. Everyone tends to know everyone else. If you are bad-mouthing (or gossiping about) someone in the community, it tends to get back to them. I know many people in my theatre community who have gossiped themselves out of work. Also worth noting, when an actor is talking smack about someone to me, I don't trust them. If they are criticizing someone else behind their back, I assume when I walk away, they will be doing the same behind mine.

So what do you do if you hear someone bad-mouthing someone else? Speak up. Tell them you are not comfortable talking about someone when they are not in the room. Calling them out almost always shuts the critics down immediately.

## Be Prepared

*"By failing to prepare, you are preparing to fail."*
*—Benjamin Franklin*

We refer to theatre as *show business* for a reason. Actors tend to remember the show part; the business part sometimes gets sidelined. Most actors are free spirits who crave a life where each day is different from the one before, but one of the crappy parts about being an actor is that there are no guarantees. Few actors can make a living doing what they love, so if you're going to be one of them, you need to be on your game.

When you are self-employed, your life becomes a series of job interviews. If you don't audition well, you're not going to get the gig, which is why it is so important for you to master the art of the audition. Part of that mastery is arriving at your audition or rehearsal prepared. Rehearsing your monologue the night before is probably not going to win you the part. Besides, preparation breeds confidence.

Theatre communities are small (even in large cities), and your audition (good or bad) will have a lasting impact. Directors tend to have excellent long-term memories, which can work for or against you. Trust me when I say:

- If you are unprepared, the director will take note.
- If you are unprepared, there are fifty actors behind you who probably *will* be prepared.
- If you are unprepared, you probably aren't going to get a callback.

Even if you aren't suitable for the role, if you make a good impression, the director may keep you in mind for another project or consider casting you in another part. Because acting is so competitive, talent alone isn't going to cut it. Preparedness and professionalism are the bare minimum for a working actor.

## Learn Your Lines!

Part of being prepared is doing your homework and knowing your lines. If you are in a scene and you are the only actor who doesn't have their lines down, you are holding everyone back, which will stress the other cast members out. Until you get that script out of your hands, you won't be able to explore freely.

To be clear, when we first let go of our security blanket (the script), it is perfectly normal to call for a line. We all call for lines, but how you call for a line is important. There is no need for you to take yourself out of the scene by looking at the stage manager. Stay engaged in the scene. Remain connected to the other actors on stage with you. And please, don't apologize! It's not a big deal, so don't make it one. If you are saying sorry every time you call for a line, you are eating up precious rehearsal time.

Also worth noting, actors often forget their lines when their blocking changes. Again, this is normal. We learn our lines from what we do (the blocking), so if what we are doing has changed, it throws us off temporarily.

Speaking of learning lines… Actors have many tricks and tips… here are some of them:

## TRY THIS:

### Writing Out Your Lines

Write them out by hand; do not type them. This will help your brain connect to the words.

### Run Lines

Run lines with another actor, NOT a friend. Have them read stage directions, etc. There are also apps out there to help you with your lines.

### Italian Run

To do an Italian run means the actors are saying their lines as quickly as possible without compromising the articulation. Do not "act" your lines. An Italian run is all about speed. When an actor makes an error, keep going back until they get it right.

### Quiz

Quiz yourself. Cover all but the line you are working on with a piece of paper. When you have mastered one line, move on to the next. Work in small sections.

### Take a Break

Take a nap or go for a walk after running lines. This will help move lines from short-term memory to long-term memory.

### Mnemonic Device

Use a mnemonic device. For example, write down the first letter of every word in your lines. This will help your recall when you see those letters on the page. Think of it as a shortcut. Example: T-B-O-N-T-B. Have you figured it out? (To be or not to be.)

### Memorize Your Cue Lines

Record the cue lines. Learn the cue lines. This will help you with speed. Also, when you look at cue lines, ask yourself what in that person's line prompts your character to speak, then highlight it. Connecting the cue line to your line will help you remember what you say next.

> **Move**
Move while you memorize. Meditation in motion helps the words stick. If you have the blocking for the scene, I recommend you run your lines with the blocking. This will help you to embody the text.

> **Memorize Before Bed**
Learn your lines before you go to sleep. Studies show this improves memory. Run lines again when you wake up the next morning. This helps the words move to long-term memory.

> **Memorize Your Punctuation**
Memorizing punctuation is as important as memorizing your lines. (See Act V: "The Play's the Thing." The Importance of Punctuation.) The playwright has provided the character with a specific rhythm or way of speaking. It is important to honour the playwright's intent.

> **Imagery**
Use imagery rather than just focusing on the words. Have one image for each thought. Think of the words as part of a story. Connecting with the story will also help with transitions. Let's be honest, memorization is boring—exploring the story is not. Connect with the story.

**The Bottom Line:**

There is no one way of learning lines that works for everyone. Experiment. Find out what method works best for you.

### Arrive on Time!

*"Early is on time, on time is late, and late is unacceptable!"*
*—Eric Dickey*

This is a big one. If you are fortunate enough to land a part, act like a pro. If you are in an acting class, a workshop or a rehearsal, demonstrate your commitment by showing up on time. Because theatre is a collaborative art form, rehearsal or training cannot begin in earnest until everyone has arrived. If you are late for an audition, they will assume you will also be late for rehearsal. When you arrive late for rehearsal, it affects the entire team. Putting the creative team behind schedule will not make you popular.

Having said that, we've all been late at one time or another—the car blows a tire, someone needs to go to the hospital in an emergency, or your cat dies. That is not what I am talking about here. Generally speaking, people who are late don't give themselves enough wiggle room to deal with life's day-to-day obstacles. Things like rush hour traffic, crappy road conditions, or finding the rehearsal hall on the first day. It has been my unfortunate experience that people who are late are consistently late. Nine times out of ten, it is the same people, with the same excuses: "I lost track of time" or "My bus was late."

In most jobs, if you are late, you can work through your lunch or work late to make up the time. In theatre, the entire team must find a way to make up that time. I cannot tell you how many insanely talented actors have blown their reputations by consistently showing up late. Besides, being late increases your stress level. Who needs that?

**The Bottom Line:**

> If you arrive fifteen minutes early, you can begin rehearsal relaxed and ready to play.

### I'm Not Working Harder Than You!

Helping my students reach their creative potential is my job. I will go to the wall for any student who is working hard. I love working with actors who are passionate about their craft. Every now and then, I get a student who wants extra help but doesn't want to put in the work themselves. They want me to do it for them.

I have no problem working as hard as you are. I will put in extra hours; I will recommend solutions. I will never give up on you unless you give up on you. Even then I'll try and convince you not to abandon ship, but *if you are expecting me to work harder than you, it's not going to happen.*

In my university class, I had one student who would always hang around after the class was over. He would always have a question or two for me. How can I improve? Who would I recommend for a film acting class? I of course, took note of this. When I asked him why he was always hanging out after class, he told me he always wants to be the last student in the room to demonstrate his commitment and passion for acting. Now this is a kid I'm going to go to the wall for!

## Respect Your Fellow Thespians

Stay far away from these three "Cs": comparing, complaining and criticizing. You can learn a great deal by watching other actors at work, whether they are beginners or seasoned actors. During the first days of rehearsal for a play I had co-written, I recall one of our theatre community's most experienced actors asking countless questions. Later that morning, on a coffee break, I overheard the younger (much less experienced) cast members secretly mocking him for wasting precious rehearsal time. I gently intervened, advising them to "watch and learn."

Over the next few weeks, those newbie actors did watch, and boy, did they learn.

For the remainder of the rehearsal period, I watched their jaws drop in awe as a complex, truthful, brilliant character was crafted before their very eyes, the result, no doubt, of countless hours of research and the many questions he dared to ask in the early stages of rehearsal.

This man was, and remains to this day, an actor who shows up every day to rehearsal with a kind word, a smile on his face and a fresh idea to explore. Although his theatre resume is incredibly impressive, he treats everyone in the room with mutual love and respect, whether it is their first show or their one hundredth. He approaches the rehearsal process as if he were an actor in his very first role. He is not only the kind of actor we should all aspire to be; he is the kind of actor directors love to hire.

P.S. Another way to show respect is to turn off your devices. There is no place for cell phones in a studio or rehearsal hall. It takes great courage to step onto that stage, especially as a developing actor, and nothing stings more than being ignored by your peers. If you have to use your phone, it's best to leave the room and return when you are finished.

### Keep Your Judgements to Yourself

*"Everything that irritates us about others can lead us to a better understanding of ourselves."* —*Carl Jung*

No one wants or benefits from judgment, so keep that in mind when watching your classmates or cast members at work. Sure, sometimes you will be learning what not to do, but that can be incredibly valuable. And isn't judging our classmates more about making ourselves feel better about our work than it is about the actor we are judging? Maybe we say out loud what we fear others may say about us when we are not in the room.

Besides, judging other people's work is not your job—we have directors for that. I say this with a wink because the best directors do not judge; they guide and inspire. And don't forget why the director is there in the first place—to direct actors! They have the training and skillset to provide constructive feedback. They have a vision for the play, and although you are an important part of that vision, they see things you cannot.

**The Bottom Line:**

Release the idea of judgement, both of yourself and others.

### Do Not Direct Other Actors

This is one of the most common boo-boos made by developing actors. They want to boss each other around, usually with good intentions. Most just want their scene to be the best it can be. At the university level, there is often the added pressure of grades. If you are paired with someone who does not share your work ethic, it can be incredibly frustrating. Whatever the reason, an actor should *never ever tell another actor what to play or how to play it.* It is not your job. Your job is to act.

If you work in a retail job and you're not the manager but start ordering other employees around, I'm guessing you won't be nominated for employee of the month. The same common sense applies here. Also, when you're playing out a scene, you probably aren't in the best position to observe, because you are incapable of watching yourself or your scene partner objectively. The best directors collaborate rather than dictate, but collaboration between you and the director means working together; it does not mean telling another actor what to do. *Let the director direct and the actors act.*

There are always exceptions to the rule. If the facilitator of a class or workshop invites students to share their feedback, that is perfectly acceptable as long as it's done constructively. Try to frame your comment in the form of a question like, "What would happen if the rhythm changed, leading to the climax?" Questions feel way less accusatory because questions are about curiosity and exploration, not judgment.

Another exception would be if you are rehearsing a scene for an acting class or workshop and no director is present. When you are left to your own devices, it is kosher to collaborate with your scene partner. Using "we" rather than "you" when making suggestions. That way, your partner isn't going to feel like they are the problem; you are exploring how to make your scene better together.

**The Bottom Line:**

> Suggestions are a great way to explore, but remember, suggesting is worlds apart from telling. If the other actor isn't open to your idea, move on.

## Be a Team Player

Theatre is a team sport; even if you are introverted (and some of the best actors are), you should bond with the group. That is not to say you need to socialize with everyone outside of rehearsal or class, but it does mean you make an effort to connect with everyone when you are together in a workspace. When a class or a cast is bonded, you can see it in their work.

When I say theatre is a team sport, that means not only connecting with cast members, it means connecting with the entire creative team: the director, assistant director, stage manager, the lighting designer, set and costume designer, even the janitor. It also helps if you connect with those who join the team late in the rehearsal process, like the running crew. Remember, the backstage crew is not there to get in your way; they are there to help you and ensure the show runs smoothly and safely. Everyone on your team deserves equal respect because the more bonded and collaborative the team, the more spectacular the show. When people feel connected and respected, they do their best work.

The team approach is also influencing how we approach the rehearsal process. Gone are the days when the director rolls into rehearsal on the first day and lays down the law. More and more university acting programs and professional theatres are adopting a work protocol with the entire cast and crew. What does a healthy work environment look like to each person? One person's idea of a respectful work environment may differ significantly from someone else's. When everyone's voice is heard and reflected in the work agreement, team members feel included and are far more likely to be on board.

## Practise the Five Pillars of Consent

Traditionally, when discussing intimacy, actors haven't had a seat at the table, which is ludicrous since the actors are the ones on the front lines. The power dynamic between actors and directors, (or actors and instructors) can be intimidating. In the past, it was assumed that actors were comfortable with touching and being touched. Because actors are trained to please, we are often expected to go beyond our comfort zone. If a director asks us to do something, we want to say yes, not only because we want the show to be the best it can be but also because we fear that if we question the direction we are given, we will be labelled as "difficult."

The good news is that the "Me Too" movement has forced the film and theatre industry to reevaluate how they work with actors. In short order, intimacy directors and coordinators have started to become invaluable in professional theatres and on film sets.

Even though we have come a long way in a short time, intimacy protocol is still evolving. Theatre schools and acting programs are playing catch-up with consent-based training. There are also many grey areas. When is an intimacy professional necessary? What is considered intimate? Some actors may think intimacy is limited to kissing and simulated sex. What about hugging? Verbally abusive dialogue? Holding hands? Is a scene with yelling and screaming considered intimate? What about pushing and shoving? A highly physical fight scene? What is comfortable for one actor may not be comfortable for another. What is non-consensual?

Because intimacy coordinators are relatively new, not all production companies and theatres are up to speed, and even if they are, small theatre companies and community theatres don't have the budget to hire them. In an ideal world, intimacy coordinators/directors would be on set or in rehearsals whenever deemed necessary, but the reality is that there will be times when actors and directors will be left to their own devices. My first-year performance students, for example, are required to rehearse their scenes outside of class. Students should avoid rehearsing intimate moments without an instructor/director present. A student may sometimes feel pressured to go along with something they aren't comfortable with. And we don't want that!

Directors, teachers and intimacy professionals need to promote a culture of consent. At the very least, actors and directors should practise the five "Cs" of consent, as recommended by the ICC (Intimacy Coordinators of Canada). These basic guidelines of safe theatre practices will promote a collaborative and consensual rehearsal environment.

**CONTEXT:** The actors should clearly understand the given circumstances of the scene and how intimacy feeds into the narrative. Before rehearsals begin, intimacy director Sharon Bajer recommends reviewing your script and flagging anything you deem intimate, including emotional and physical intimacy.

She also advises that you write down all your questions. Be specific. For instance, if there is a kiss, what kind of kiss will it be? On the cheek? On the mouth? Will the mouth be opened or closed? Is it fast and hard? How long will the kiss last? Are you comfortable with your scene partner putting their hands around your waist before the kiss? During the kiss? There are so many questions!

In the past, these decisions were often made by the director. Intimacy awareness takes out all of the guesswork. There is no need to make it up as you go along. Rather than being told what will happen, you can actively participate in the decision-making. It should be a collaborative effort. At the end of the day, you are the one on stage doing it. You need to be the boss of your own body and emotions.

**COMMUNICATION:** If there is no budget for an intimacy coordinator, the director should establish an open discussion about intimacy. If they don't, by all means raise the issue! Make sure all your questions are answered before giving consent. Discuss how you would like to approach the scenario and what each actor is comfortable with. You may not want your hair to be touched, or you may not want another actor's hands near your neck.

Or it may be a wardrobe issue. Say something if you discover the skirt you tried on in a costume fitting now feels too restrictive or revealing. Don't suffer in silence. A good director wants you to be comfortable on stage. Communication should remain open throughout the rehearsal process and beyond. Once the show is up, there should be regular check-ins.

**CONSENT:** Consent is essential. Being able to say no matters. Think about it this way: What if your roommate helps themself to the groceries you just bought, and doesn't bother to ask you? You would be pretty pissed off, wouldn't you? Even if you agree, there may be conditions. Maybe you permit some part of the request but not all. You may, for example, say yes to staple items like butter or sugar, but nothing else.

Be proactive rather than reactive. Whether in an acting class or rehearsal, the cast and creative team should begin with an open discussion on the rules of engagement. Consent should never be assumed.

To echo intimacy director Sharon Bajer again, it should be "specific, informed and flexible. Consent given one day does not necessarily mean consent the next." Maybe you agreed to being pushed against a wall on Monday, and by the time Tuesday rolls around, you are having second thoughts. You should be able to change your mind, without retribution.

Most of the time, the director and actors can put their heads together to come up with a compromise that makes everyone happy. If that isn't the case, maybe you should reconsider whether you want to be a part of the production.

Sharon also advocates that consent should be given without pressure, force, or manipulation. If an intimacy practitioner is present, remember that they are not only there to guide you through all those uncomfortable, emotionally charged moments but also to advocate for you. If, for example, you need to clear the room while rehearsing an intimate moment, don't be afraid to say so.

> I remember being cast in a music video where I was wearing only a bra and underwear for the entire seven hours we were shooting. Not only was I cold, but I felt extremely exposed wearing next to nothing in a room with twenty people I didn't know. I was in my twenties at the time and felt too intimidated to ask if the room could be cleared. #MeToo

CHOREOGRAPHY: Think about intimate choreography the same way as you think about dance or fight choreography. Take the emotion out of the equation.

Actors have the right to know *specifically* what will happen and when. No surprises. No winging it. And absolutely no choreography until the actor has given consent.

When you begin rehearsal, if there is intimate choreography, like a slap, a kiss or a hug, I suggest saying the choreography out loud rather than doing it. An actor may gesture a slap and say, "I slap you" or "I kiss you passionately." Use language that is present tense. This allows the actor to ease in. Once you are more comfortable with the scene, the director can schedule a choreography session to give the scene the time and attention it deserves.

**CLOSURE:** Closure is important. After rehearsing physical or emotional choreography, a step-out ritual can be helpful. High fiving your scene partner, running through a secret handshake sequence, or connecting with your breath is usually enough to bring us back to the real world. Everyone's needs are different. If your scene partner isn't interested, devise your own. Shake your body out like a wet dog or jump around and touch your face. Make sound. Whatever works for you. And you don't have to wait until rehearsal is over either; you can step out anytime. Once you have completed your step out, take a little break and jump back in when ready. Following a show, you may want to do the same.

Familiarity with the Five "Cs" is in no way a substitute for an intimacy director. The safe practices I have shared here are only a guide meant to empower you to speak up when asked to do something you are uncomfortable with.

**The Bottom Line:**

> Full body autonomy means that only you can decide if someone touches your body or how and where they touch you, without pressure. Modifying a scene to make the actor more comfortable should always be an option. It is your right to be heard.

# ACT II: GETTING OUT OF YOUR OWN WAY

## Scene i

### EMBRACE YOUR FEAR AND CELEBRATE YOUR FAILURE

*"Anyone who has never made a mistake has never tried anything new." —Albert Einstein*

I wanted to begin this book by addressing the most significant obstacle standing in the way of you reaching your full acting potential—***fear.*** Doing our best work, particularly in auditions, is virtually impossible if our minds and bodies are not fully relaxed. But how can our bodies be relaxed when we are overwhelmed with fear? To make matters worse, the more we try to will those nasty emotions away, the more they seem to metastasize.

### You Are Not Alone

*"Find out what a person fears most and that is where he will develop next."—Carl Jung*

When fear grabs hold of you and won't let go, it is helpful to remember that ***you are not alone.***

For some reason, most of us believe we are the only ones in the room feeling fear, which couldn't be further from the truth. We may feel different types of fear, but we all feel it at one time or another.

That is why, on the first day of every acting class I teach, I hand each student a blank slip of paper and ask them to write down their greatest fear in signing up for my class. I then assure them that their responses will remain anonymous. When they are finished writing, we (including me) put our pieces of paper in a hat. Then, everyone draws one slip (not their own) and reads it aloud to the class. Although I have done this exercise hundreds of times, the answers never fail to break my heart. My students write things like: "I fear embarrassing myself." "I fear I will not fit in." "I fear I have no talent." "I fear I will disappoint the rest of the cast." I know, right? Pretty heart-wrenching stuff.

I get it. All those fears are fears that I have experienced. How we respond to that fear determines whether we conquer fear or fear conquers us.

**The Bottom Line:**

> Courage doesn't mean you're not afraid; it means you are afraid and do it anyway.

### Fear Itself?

*"Courage is resistance to fear, mastery of fear, not absence of fear."*
*—Mark Twain*

Fear is universal. As long as you live and breathe, you will experience fear. And that's okay, because fear serves a purpose. It's a safety mechanism that warns us of potential danger, protects us from harm, and prevents us from doing really stupid things.

Fear is also a great motivator. When a show is a week away from opening and the actors haven't got their lines down, or haven't been fully present in rehearsal, it is fear that drives them to the finish line. Without fear, we probably wouldn't get much done.

And isn't it impossible to quash our fear anyway? In my experience, telling my students to stop being afraid only increases their anxiety. We feel what we feel—someone telling us to "fear not" isn't going to change that. The truth is, fear is inevitable, so go on and feel your fear. Besides, fear is not the problem. It is what we do with it that matters. If you live your life in fear of losing, you are setting yourself up for failure.

When I think of fear, Franklin Delano Roosevelt's famous words from his first inaugural speech immediately come to mind: "The only thing we have to fear is fear itself." Although the next part of the sentence in his famous address is often overlooked, it is of particular interest to our discussion here:

Let me assert my firm belief that the only thing we have to fear is fear itself—nameless, unreasoning, unjustified terror which paralyzes needed efforts to convert retreat into advance.

**The Bottom Line:**

> FDR is saying there is nothing inherently wrong with fear as long as we can find a way to turn that retreat into an advance.

## Own Your Fear

*"Failure must be shared. This is an imperative. Spare no information in the telling. And always endeavour to tell the person you would least want to tell." —Sarah Garton Stanley*

One of the first steps in turning that retreat into an advance is to own your fear. You know what they say, "Don't run away from an angry bear." First of all, you may trip and become a quick forest lunch. Then, because the bear (fear monster) senses your fear, it will consider you an easy target. Slowly make your move, back away with confidence, telling yourself, like that bear, you were meant to be here. You will have to share the stage…forest…with each other. Next time you meet, say, "Hey, Bear, I remember you from the last time we met! I know how to make my way outta here, thankyouverymuch!"

Allow me to share a story about the power of owning your fear. On the first day of a master-level boot camp for actors at Simon Fraser University in British Columbia, the participants were all asked to gather in a circle on the floor. The head guru then asked us to share our greatest fear going into the intensive with the group. Since the participants had just arrived from all across Canada and the U.S., most of us hadn't even had the chance to say hello. Under the circumstances, the guru's question was a very intimidating ask. "You want me to admit my greatest fear to a room full of strangers? Not going to happen!" My walls immediately went up.

When it was my turn to speak, I somehow mustered enough courage to admit my fear, and surprisingly, so did most of my classmates, all but one. One of the participants claimed she feared nothing. Immediately, I sensed she was not being honest and unfortunately, as the weeks unfolded, my suspicions were confirmed. It turns out that she feared just about everything. Ultimately, she made little progress, not because she wasn't talented, but because she spent the entire time resisting. She closed all the doors when our purpose in being there was to open them.

I say all this, knowing that even though I could admit my fear on that first day, I spent the first week of five doing precisely what that woman had done—resisting everything. In order to protect myself, I was putting up one wall after the other. What was I so afraid of anyway? Honestly? The answer to this unwelcome question was fear of failure, fear of being made fun of, and fear of not measuring up. But what I learned is that my fear of failure was far more terrifying than the failure itself.

The only difference between that student and me was that once I built trust with my mentors, my walls of resistance began to melt away like Chapstick in the car in July. By acknowledging my fear and realizing my mentor's sole purpose was to make me a better actor and not humiliate me, I could move through my fear to the other side.

I wish I could tell you that the anxiety I was experiencing magically disappeared, but it didn't. It remained with me for the entire five weeks, but with each day, there was less of it. As the days wore on, and I continued to bring my fear along for the ride, there was much more advancing and much less retreating. Now that's progress!

**The Bottom Line:**

Own your fear. Say it out loud (maybe not in public). Being honest with yourself will weaken fear's hold over you.

## Be a Trier

*"Our doubts are traitors and make us lose the good we oft might win by fearing to attempt."* —*Willy the Shake,* Measure for Measure

Avoid judging your work, particularly in the beginning. We all want to master our craft immediately, but that isn't going to happen. Just show up and do the work. Good, bad, who cares? Let it go. It's none of your business. You don't have a crystal ball, so why not let go of the result?

To confront fear is to open your heart to possibility. In the words of one of my favourite Canadian playwrights, George F. Walker: "Be a trier!" What is the alternative? If you don't try, you are treading water with no possibility of advancement. The universe loves a trier! Just the act of trying builds confidence. So why not be a trier?

We all know people who are not triers. They are the ones who are no fun at parties. They choose to observe rather than participate. They are the roommates who refuse to try ketchup on their mac and cheese! And really, how do they know they won't like it if they have never tried it?

"I just know," they say. What if they ate it and hated it? At least they can call themselves a trier. If it tastes like crap, they can scrape that mac and cheese off their plate and into the garbage can.

Then they can say, "No, thank you, roommate. I tried that mac and cheese with ketchup, and it's not for me!" or at least, "It's not for me right now." If they love it, they are the beneficiaries! Your next debate can be Heinz versus French's.

In the words of Eleanor Roosevelt, "Do one thing that scares you every day." Put yourself in vulnerable scenarios. For instance, if I sign up for an improv workshop with rockstar improvisers (which I am not) I will seek out the best improviser in the room to partner with because I know that the more expertise they have, the more I'm going to learn. Not only that, if I only act with less talented people, I am cheating myself. I want to play on the all-star team, because it is bound to make me better. I am not taking a workshop to show off the skills I already have, I am taking it to acquire new ones. Besides, what is left to fear once you work with the most talented person in the room?

When we refuse to try, most, if not all, those refusals are based on fear. I see you! You didn't go out for that audition because you feared you wouldn't win the part. But what if you did? And, even if you didn't, you may have missed out on the worst audition of your life, and the worst audition means the next one is going to be better. The most disheartening, painful choice is not to audition at all.

Trying is certainly more exciting than sitting back and letting the world pass you by. It's always more life-affirming to be a participant, rather than an observer. You might have more scars than the observers of the world, but damn it, you'll know you're alive.

**The Bottom Line:**

> Acting is a risky business. It's like skydiving—you don't know where you are going to land. And let's not downplay the jumping out of a plane part, it's pretty scary stuff. At the end of the day, you're either going to take that leap of faith and jump out of that plane, or you're going to sit on the sidelines wishing you did.

### TRY THIS:

> **Take a risk.**
Start with something small, like taking an unfamiliar route to a familiar destination or having chocolate cake for breakfast instead of bran flakes. Then, step it up. (Nothing that puts your safety at risk.) If starting a conversation with a stranger is hard for you, make your move. Eventually, you will find the courage to take that risk-taking to the stage.

### AND THIS:

The next time your acting teacher asks who's up for some improv, even if you would rather have a root canal (which, by the way, means you need to get up and do improv), force your hand in the air and holler, "Pick me!" When you say "pick me" out loud, you are defying fear by doing it anyway. And fear doesn't like that one little bit.

## Celebrate Your Failure!

*"Success consists of going from failure to failure without loss of enthusiasm." —Winston Churchill*

To celebrate failure with fervour, we must first rewrite our old-school notions of fear. Sarah Garton Stanley highlights how messed up our modern view of failure is in her thirteen-point Manifesto on Failure. "Success gets a party; it's time to give failure a wake." I couldn't agree more! We see failure as this horrible, shameful thing because our culture celebrates success rather than failure, when it should be the other way around.

Sarah's manifesto got me thinking about my theatre school experience and its paralyzing fear of failure. Looking back, I wondered if there were any moments in those four years of training when I didn't feel that way. The answer was "Yes!" when I registered for Rick Skene's Mime and Improv class.

It wasn't enough that I had a debilitating fear of improv. Rick would give us some terrifying assignments, like creating a solo mime piece in five minutes—on the first day! Worse, he would make us perform it in front of the class! He might as well have given me a death sentence. A minute in, my panic meter started to rise, and my heart felt like it might leap out of my chest. Sheer terror ensued.

How in the hell was I supposed to create a life-changing piece of theatre with only five minutes on the clock and without any words or a scene partner to blame it on when it all went to hell? The only saving grace was that five minutes didn't give me much time to overthink. Somehow, I had to get out of my head and into my body. This was life or death (or at least it felt that way at the time) Out of utter desperation, I chose life, and truth be told, eight times out of ten, the pieces would suck, but every now and then, a glimmer of brilliance would find its way to the stage.

Rick was trying to teach us to celebrate failure, and he created an environment that encouraged it. The entire class became so enthusiastic about falling flat on our faces that we invented our very own "tunnel of shame." (An area in the studio flanked on both sides by black curtains.) If you knew your work was garbage, immediately following your performance, you would make a beeline for the "tunnel," head hanging dramatically low, tail between your legs, all the while your classmates clapping and cheering you on.

Freedom to fail was the greatest gift he could have given me. Never in my life had I been given permission to fail. Damn, it felt good! And who knew failure could be so much fun? But why was it fun? Instead of dreading failure, we started to look forward to it. More importantly, it was self-imposed. It wasn't our peers or our instructor shaming us or telling us we sucked; it was us owning our failure. Rick turned our studio into a playground where a class of scared-stiff theatre students was transformed into a room full of risk-takers.

Whether you are practising law, medicine or acting, metaphorically skinning your knee is inevitable. That is why we refer to it as a practice. If you aren't falling, you aren't learning—***the more you fall, the more you learn.*** You wouldn't go to the ice rink for the first time, throw on a pair of skates, and expect to skate like an Olympian, would you? Of course not! You would expect to fall a lot, because you have to fall to learn how to skate. And if someday your passion leads to competitive skating, you would have to accept that failure would be an essential part of your journey.

Acting is no different. You must be willing to be bad before you will be good. That brilliant ice-skating Olympian was once a terrible skater. It's true! When they were learning to skate, they fell a thousand times. As they got better and started to learn technique, there was a lot more falling.

To master their craft, they would have to dedicate hundreds, maybe even thousands, of hours to failing.

This is true not only for acting and ice skating; it's true of everything! Let me also say, ***there is no more motivating force for change than failure.*** Successful people are the people who are most willing to fail their way to success. ***Without failure, success is not possible.***

And in those rare moments when we are basking in the afterglow of our success, we must remember that failure is coming for us. And that's okay because ***even though success leads to failure, failure also leads to success.*** On a good day, we are hovering somewhere between the two.

And one more thing, if you're going to fail, why not fail epically? It needs to hurt, and it needs to hurt a lot. The bigger the failure, the bigger the gain. If you fall and skin your knee, dust yourself off and can get on with your day like nothing happened, you are probably not failing big enough. To steal from Sarah again, she argues, "*Once felt … I can assure you that it is an experience you really cannot wait to look back on. It is rear-view mirror learning at its very best.*" To inspire change, you need to throw yourself at failure. You need to fail so hard that you don't think you will be able to get back up. ***It is the most debilitating failure that will teach you the most.***

### The Bottom Line:

> If you fail, you're still a good person! All of us will experience a lot more failure than we will success. So please, emerging thespians, bring on the failure! The more, the better! Skin those knees and skin them often. I promise a scab will form, and a thicker layer of skin will take its place.

## Scene ii

### BUILDING AND MAINTAINING CONFIDENCE

### Stop Bad-Mouthing Yourself!

*"Be careful how you are talking to yourself because you are listening"—Hayes*

I'm not sure why we are so hard on ourselves, but most of us are, especially actors. Negative self-talk may be all the rage, but it needs to stop because it wounds. Sometimes, it leaves scar tissue. It's like a tattoo you changed your mind about and now want to erase. Sure, you can do it, but it's going to take time; it's going to be painful, and it will leave its mark on you. So stop it. Right now. Period. From now on, ban yourself from talking smack about *you*. Seriously!

**The Bottom Line:**

You wouldn't bad-mouth your best friend, so why bad-mouth yourself?

**TRY THIS:**
Every time you are about to drive down Negative Highway, slam on the brakes and point yourself in the opposite direction.

### Affirm Yourself

To turn your thought process around, you must find some nice things to say about yourself.

And don't tell me there isn't anything nice to say because I don't believe you! I accept that this may be challenging for some of you, not because you have no talent, but because you may not believe the words coming out of your mouth. And that's okay. I'm not asking you to believe. Yet. I'm asking you to say it. Believing can come later.

When I first started positive self-talk, it felt insincere, alien, even. I wasn't used to talking nicely to myself. Because I had been bad-mouthing myself since puberty, those negative thoughts weren't just going to exit stage right. It would require a heavy dose of persistence, like a dog after a bone. Go after that bone. Use your affirmations to fight back. If someone was saying cruel things about someone you love, would you sit back and say nothing? Of course, you wouldn't. You would stand up for them. It's time to stand up for yourself!

Standing up for yourself also means reframing how you see yourself. I have ADHD. I am not a victim of anything; I am a survivor. ADHD is a gift, not a disability. Where some people can only see one answer, I can see many. I may be easily distracted, but when I am passionate about something (like theatre), I can hyper-focus in a way most other people cannot. This has been incredibly useful to me as a playwright. Sounds more like a gift than a disability to me.

**The Bottom Line:**

Affirmations are a powerful weapon in the war against self-hate. And you can win that war.

**TRY THIS:**

Your own words can be weaponized against you. Retaliate by saying something incredibly nice about yourself instead. Say it. And keep saying it. Until you believe it. Promise yourself that from now on, you will only talk to yourself like you would talk to someone you love.

*Here's a few to get you started:* (Say your affirmation out loud a minimum of three times.)

- I embrace challenges as opportunities.
- Rejection is a great teacher.
- I am unique.
- Acting is my calling.
- The role is within me.
- Each audition makes me a better auditioner.

- Today, I will do one thing that will bring me one step closer to my dream.

### Surround Yourself with Cheerleaders

*"A friend is someone who knows you as you are, understands where you have been, accepts what you have become, and still, gently allows you to grow."—Willy the Shake*

While on your acting journey, it is essential that you feel safe and accepted. Family and friends may make negative comments out of concern. Well-meaning parents may worry that you won't be able to make a decent living, or a spouse may feel threatened that your passion for theatre will consume you and exclude them. Friends may feel threatened or jealous because they secretly wish they dared to take an artistic leap. Outsiders may say things like, "Acting is a hobby, not a profession."

Whatever your loved ones have to say, don't let their fear derail you. Protect your inner artist at all costs. Only allow those who love and support you to remain in your inner circle. We underestimate the effect of toxic people in our lives. Isn't dealing with our own self-sabotage enough? Why add to it? If someone makes you feel bad about yourself all the time, or if you feel like you are continually defending yourself whenever you are around that person, you may want to reconsider having them in your life.

It's hard when it's family (we don't get to choose them), so you may have to limit your time with them rather than cancel them entirely. And remember, just because you remove someone from your inner circle today doesn't mean that they are banished forever. If things change, you can welcome that person back into your fold. If not, arrivederci!

How can you detox with toxic people in your life? The short answer is you can't. You should wear your inner circle like a warm blanket on a frigid Canadian winter day. The genuinely supportive people in your life will always offer you a soft place to fall.

**TRY THIS:**

List the people in your life who least support you. For the next month, distance yourself from them. Write down how their absence affects you. Do you miss them? Do you feel lighter? Freer to express yourself? More confident?

**AND THIS:**

Now, make a list of the people who are most enthusiastic and supportive about your acting. When they are around, do you feel more centred and confident? Rejuvenated?

What does that tell you?

**AND THIS:**

Draw a circle. Put your name smack dab in the middle of the circle. Write the names of your supportive teachers, friends and family inside the circle. Write the names of the toxic people on the outside. Look at this drawing whenever you doubt your artistry.

Let this be a reminder of who is poison and who is not.

**The Bottom Line:**

Confident people surround themselves with cheerleaders.

## Banish All Toxic Teachers

*"An understanding heart is everything in a teacher and cannot be esteemed highly enough. One looks back with appreciation to the brilliant teachers, but with gratitude to those who touched our human feeling."—Carl Jung*

Let's briefly discuss toxic teachers. My immediate response to all the dream-crushers out there can be summed up in the words of Vincent Van Gogh, "If someone tells you you can't paint, paint." In the past, whenever I encountered a toxic teacher, I would use it for fuel. It would fire me up. Instead of walking away, I would double down, determined to prove them wrong. Now I would opt for an easier solution: Banish that teacher and never look back.

Most acting professors and instructors are warm, caring, kind and inspiring. They build trust with their students and create a safe space for their students to explore and grow. Unfortunately, I have also heard far too many stories of teachers who use humiliation as a teaching technique, in some cases telling students that acting is not for them or calling them out in an embarrassing manner in front of their peers. THAT SHOULD NEVER HAPPEN! That tells us more about them than it does about you.

There is a big difference between challenging a student and humiliating them. If a teacher has earned your trust, they can dig deeper. They can challenge you. A good teacher's goal is always to help their student improve and gain confidence. Humiliation should NEVER be used as a teaching strategy.

Once trust between the actor and the teacher has been built, most students will willingly venture outside of their comfort zone. I have yet to meet a student who didn't blossom by being in an acting class or a show with a loving teacher or director. I have yet to meet a student who flourished in a toxic environment.

**The Bottom Line:**

If an instructor is good at what they do, students past and present will gush about them.

**TRY THIS:**

The best way to find a gifted teacher is to ask around. Who do others recommend and why? Did they have fun in the class? (And yes, having fun is critical because if you are having a good time, you are more likely to put yourself out there.) Were they challenged? Did they grow as a result? The majority of the students who sign up for my classes find their way to me through referrals.

## Waste No Time on Crap You Have Zero Control Over

*"God grant me the serenity to accept the things I cannot change, the courage to change the things I can, and the wisdom to know the difference." —Reinhold Niebuhr*

Most of you are familiar with the Serenity Prayer. Although it was popularized by Alcoholics Anonymous, the prayer's universal message of acceptance and surrender is particularly relevant to the developing actor.

When I'm ready to throw in the towel after the tenth rejection letter arrives in my inbox, or I don't get a callback after yet another film audition, I recite it aloud to remind me to soldier on.

There are so many things beyond an actor's control: whether you get that callback, vocal range, appearance, typecasting, and even talent. So why worry about it? Why worry about things you have no control over? If all that worry were going to change the outcome miraculously, it would make sense, but if not, it's a complete waste of time and energy. All that worrying will cost you big time because it will slowly eat away at your soul and destroy your confidence.

Accept that you don't know what the outcome will be. Let go of the result! Wow, that takes a lot of weight off your shoulders, doesn't it? And what's so bad about not knowing anyway? Life would be kind of dull if we always knew what was coming next. I don't know of any actor that has much of an idea of what is coming next. Will I be cast in the movie I auditioned for? Is that new artistic director going to hire me for one of the shows in their season? How about that national television commercial I auditioned for? You don't know. Actors spend a lot of time not knowing, which is why your parents want you to become a chartered accountant instead of an actor!

Although I have no control over whether the Arts Council awards me a playwriting grant, whether the publisher publishes my work, or whether I'm cast in a movie, I do have control over how I respond. I can write and practise my craft; I can submit my play to another publisher, and I can arrive more prepared for my next audition.

I know what all you worriers are saying to yourself right now: "If I could do that, I would do that!" Some of you can't help yourself. Worrying is in your DNA. The question then becomes, "How do I turn my retreat into an advance?" The answer is simple: replace all that worry with something more productive.

**The Bottom Line:**

Change what is changeable. Forget the rest.

**TRY THIS:**

Labour on your ability to pick up a scene cold and get to the heart of it; hone your improvisational skills or take a cooking class. These things will not only take your mind off the minutiae but will also make you a better actor and a more well-rounded person, which will also make you a better actor.

## Live Your Life in the Present

*"I am not what happened to me; I am what I choose to become"*
*—Carl Jung*

There are so many benefits to learning how to live your life in the present. Instead of wasting time and energy reliving an imperfect childhood, obsessing over how many likes you have on Instagram, or worrying about what will happen next week or five minutes from now, you can embrace the moment you are in.

Wow! Sounds pretty liberating, doesn't it? No more anxiety or stress worrying about something that has already happened, or something about to happen—you are free to just BE. Phew! I bet you feel better already!

P.S. That does not mean you shouldn't reflect and learn from past experiences or forget about paying your bills or booking an audition. It just means you should pay the bills, pick up the phone and book that audition so that you can remain present in your life. Doing is active. Doing is present.

**The Bottom Line:**

We must refuse to allow our past to consume our present and dictate our future. Being present in your life will translate to being present on stage.

### Stop Talking and Start Walking!

*"How soon 'not now' becomes 'never.'" —Martin Luther King*

Procrastination is a confidence killer. It makes us feel bad. It makes us feel guilty, and it steals our energy. Fighting against it is no easy task. Sometimes, particularly with longer-term goals, it's hard to stay motivated—enthusiasm wanes. Or maybe your procrastination is wrapped in a blanket of fear. Either way, even the worker bees among us have moments where we are spinning our tires. Although I cannot promise to eliminate your procrastination, I can offer up some strategies that have worked for me—the rest is up to you.

One of the most effective solutions for combating procrastination is ***immediate action***. Instead of allowing your brain time to conjure up a gazillion excuses not to act on your creative inspiration, act. Do something. Now. Do one simple thing that brings you closer to that goal before you allow those nasty inner voices to hijack your creative impulse.

In my case, it meant sitting down at my computer and putting some words on the page. I told myself to act—NOW—and here I am, writing this book! Most of the time, when we don't follow through on something, it is because we fear failure.

Like Rick Skene's Mime and Improv class, immediate action doesn't allow you to overthink. How often have you talked about doing something and not followed through? We are "all talk and no action," as they say, but as we all know, talking about something doesn't make it happen. ***We need to walk the walk, rather than just talking the talk.*** Acting on an impulse also builds confidence and reduces stress.

But what in the world does walking the walk have to do with acting? Everything! As an actor, you must train your brain to act on instinct. To take risks and let go of the result. If you don't take the risk, isn't that failure? A failure to launch? Your brain can be your best friend or worst enemy. If you overthink everything, you are killing your creative impulses.

Usually, our instincts lead us in the right direction, but more often than not, we slam the door. We may claim that we "don't feel like it." The truth is, you're never going to "feel like it." Rather than overthink, go ahead and sign up for that acting workshop, book that audition, or begin writing that play! If you want to try something new in rehearsal, don't save it—do it. Listen to your inner voice and then act on it ***immediately.***

In writing this book, for instance, it was easy to talk myself out of it. And truth be told, sometimes I did. "I'm just not feeling inspired today," I would say. "I'll get back at it first thing tomorrow." Of course, tomorrow would come and go. In my heart, I knew if I continued to be seduced by that overpowering censor in my head, the book would never get written.

When I finally grew sick and tired of my procrastination, I devised a plan I could live with: I made a contract with myself that I would write for one hour every day, seven days a week—NO MATTER WHAT. Every day (okay, almost every day) after that, I set my alarm for sixty minutes, sat at my computer, and put some words on the page.

My alarm is set as I am writing this sentence. When that alarm goes off, I will finish the sentence I am writing and put it away. Done. Success! Although I am a huge fan of embracing failure, goldang it, small successes feel good! And that little dopamine hit is enough to bring me back the next day.

Even when my schedule is overwhelming, I show up on the page. If I have to wake up at five a.m. to squeeze it into my schedule, I show up on the page. If I have to write in an airport between flights, I show up on the page. If I have to divide my writing time into two thirty-minute sessions, I show up on the page. The most shocking part? It's not that hard! I can commit to just about anything for an hour! Sure, some days, the writing is crap, but I show up anyway. And it works! And I think it works because it's doable.

I'm not trying to write a book in a week or even six months. Truthfully, I have no idea how long this will take, and that's okay (I have a very kind and patient editor.) The important thing is I am moving forward each and every day.

The key is to take baby steps. It's kind of like buying a gym membership. When we first sign up, we are bursting at the seams with enthusiasm. We fantasize about those abs of steel we are going to have. We buy ourselves a new bathing suit. We vow to hit the gym five days a week until we look like a supermodel. And it works—for a couple of weeks.

Then reality sets in. Unless we plan never to eat again, quit our jobs, suffer from sleep deprivation and forfeit our social life, there is no way we are going to make it to the gym that often. Instead of committing to three weekly gym visits, we overcommit and end up not going at all. I see you, over-committers! You are why gyms across this country are packed in January and look like ghost towns by February. But we know you'll be back again next January. And so the cycle continues. Why? Because we live in this microwave society where we want it now, and it's just not realistic.

Attempting to jump to the finish line never works. So, instead of over-promising or throwing your hands in the air and doing nothing (which eats up more time and energy than doing the thing you are procrastinating about), commit yourself one hundred percent for a designated period and then walk away. That way, you'll feel good. If you're procrastinating, you're treading water (sometimes even doing the backstroke), and that will make you feel like crap. And while you're waiting for inspiration to make her appearance (which seldom happens), someone who "doesn't feel like it" is doing it anyway.

**The Bottom Line:**

Act on your creative impulses immediately. If you hesitate, chances are, you'll talk yourself out of it.

### TRY THIS:

The next time you have a creative impulse, immediately act upon that idea bubbling up inside of you. Now, I don't mean reckless impulses. Your impulse should be tied to a goal. If you have an impulse to rob a bank, it's probably not a good idea, but if you want to start an improv troupe, get on the phone and find yourself a band of like-minded thespians.

If you have a long-term goal, break it down into small steps. Tackle those steps in a way that is doable for you. Then, make it a habit.

⚠ **WARNING:**
When we smell success, we often sabotage our movement forward. Success, after all, comes with expectations. Each step forward brings new challenges. Often, when we are a breath away from finding a new level of excellence, we throw in the towel. But why?

When we reach a certain skill level, maybe the compliments are not coming as often as they used to, or maybe we fear failure so intensely that we unconsciously avoid reaching for further success. Although staying where you are may feel safe, the status quo prevents you from moving forward.

## Be Resilient

*"Success is not final, failure is not fatal: it is the courage to continue that counts."—Winston Churchill*

Let's talk about resilience. If you don't have it, you need to find a way to cultivate it, because resilience is the key to your well-being and longevity as an actor. It is no accident that people drawn to an artistic life have often experienced a great deal of adversity. That adversity is your driving force. To portray a complex range of human behaviour, you have to have lived a little. The more you experience life, the better you will be at capturing it honestly.

Remember, adversity is nothing new. We have all experienced it. You, and only you, can turn that retreat into an advance. Even the best hitters in professional baseball get a hit only about three times out of every ten appearances at the plate. The actor most willing to step back into the batter's box after striking out is the actor I want to watch on stage and the actor I want to work with. And it is not enough to return to the plate, either; one must do so with enthusiasm.

P.S. There is a reason why actors refer to acting as a *process*. Respect the process. Two steps forward and one step back is still one step forward.

**The Bottom Line:**

> When we examine the mindsets of the most successful people, whether they are CEOs, athletes, or actors, it is resilience that sets them apart.

## You Are Not an Imposter

> *"All the world's a stage, and all the men and women merely players."—Willy the Shake,* As You Like It, *Act II, Scene VII*

Another obstacle on our path to building confidence is imposter syndrome. Despite excelling at what you do, do you ever feel like a phony? Like you don't deserve what you have worked so hard to achieve? For a long time, I believed that I was alone in feeling this way, but when I talked to other people, most of us were singing the same song. Turns out, most of us feel like an imposter at some point in our lives. Me included.

Although my career was successful, I always felt like I was living someone else's life. That at any moment, someone would discover my dirty little secret—that I was pretending to be someone I am not. I can't call myself a playwright! Having a couple of plays produced and published doesn't make me a playwright. So what if I won an award for my playwriting? I can't call myself a writer! A degree in acting doesn't make me an actor! Who do I think I am, opening up a theatre school? And what in the hell is going to happen when they find out I'm a fraud?

**The Bottom Line:**

> If you are in the process of writing a play, or you have written a play, or if you are taking a playwriting class, then you are a playwright. Period. You are a writer of plays, a

wordsmith. Similarly, if you act, you are an actor. If you direct a play, you are a director. If you make a film, you are a filmmaker. Don't let anyone tell you differently.

**TRY THIS:**
Say it! Go on! I dare you! Say it loud and proud. "I AM AN ACTOR!" Saying it out loud makes it so!

## Scene iii

## NURTURING YOUR ARTIST

### Work Like a Dog & Play Like a Puppy

*"Striving for success without hard work is like trying to harvest where you haven't planted."—Charles Dickens*

You may have zero control over your talent, but you have one hundred percent control over how hard you work. Practice, failure, and persistence equal success. Lin-Manuel Miranda's Broadway hit *Hamilton* is a prime example of all three. Most people think Miranda's musical was an overnight success. It took him seven years to write his masterpiece—seven long years. Talk about persistence! This show is heralded as the most popular and profitable musical ever, winning a Pulitzer Prize, an Emmy, three Tonys and three Grammys.

But Miranda didn't appear out of nowhere and collect his prize. He didn't sit around waiting for someone to cast him in a juicy role either; he wrote one for himself. He not only worked like a dog, but he also faced a truckload of rejection, most notably from Stephen Sondheim, the most influential American composer and lyricist of the twentieth century. Sondheim told Miranda his musical didn't have a shot in hell. Did that stop him? No! Make no mistake, this man is incredibly gifted, but without Miranda's hard work and perseverance, *Hamilton* would never have made it to Broadway.

In theatre school, I remember being told repeatedly that acting is 20% talent and 80% hard work. I don't know if I fully believed it then, but I do now. I have always adopted a strong work ethic, believing that if I worked hard enough, I could accomplish anything. And I still believe this to be true.

My university students who spend the most time in the studio rehearsing and honing their skills tend to have the strongest scenes. Those who lack commitment and put in minimal effort tend to have the weakest scenes. There is no mystery here. It is the Lin-Manuel Mirandas of the world who put hundreds, if not thousands, of hours into practising their craft, who master it, right?

Yes…and no. What I wasn't told in theatre school is how important it is to play as hard as you work. Without life balance, we put our mental health and general state of well-being in jeopardy, which, in turn, hurts our work.

I used to be a full-on believer in the all-work and no-play philosophy. When I was away from work, I took it with me. I could only talk about theatre if I were out for dinner with friends.

In the middle of a yoga class, my thoughts would inevitably drift to all the work that wasn't getting done while I was "wasting time" at the yoga studio. Even when I was at the park playing with my kids, my mind would be busy preparing for the next day's rehearsal.

I didn't realize that my work obsession wasn't sustainable. Like the Energizer bunny, I worked until my battery life was spent. Then, while finishing a final draft of a play I was co-writing, I hit the wall. It was not good timing either—we were a month away from a full production. I remember sitting in front of my computer and watching the sun come up with a blank screen staring back at me. It didn't matter how hard I tried to find the words or how many tears I shed; the screen remained blank.

But failure is a great teacher! I was no longer present in my life. Not only that, I was also miserable. Working like a dog was no longer working for me. For Lin-Manuel Miranda to work as hard as he did, for as long as he did, he had to find a work-life balance, and so did I.

And so I did: Never again would my identity be solely defined by what I do. While I remain deeply passionate about what I do, "workaholic" is no longer a word in my vocabulary. It's a powerful thing to find something that you are passionate about, but that something shouldn't be your whole world.

Most artists at the top of their game work hard and play harder. They go out with friends, spend time with their families, and have romantic somebodies. They go on vacation and take long walks, they play guitar, bake cookies, and read books. They make room in their lives to recharge.

Acting is playing. Playing feeds our souls and stimulates our imagination. Taking a salsa class, going out for dinner with friends or spending a weekend at the cabin with your family is in no way going to take away from your artistry—it will enhance it. If you don't "play," it's like having a bucket of water with a hole in it. You will never be able to fill it.

**The Bottom Line:**

Achieving a healthy balance between your professional and personal life is crucial for creative fulfillment and long-term sustainability.

**TRY THIS:**

Make a list of twenty fun things you would like to do with friends, family or your special somebody. Knock one off the list each week.

*Here are a few suggestions to get you started:*

- Go ice skating with a group of friends
- Have coffee with a friend you haven't seen for a long time
- Go to a music festival
- Throw a dinner party

- Rent an Airbnb and go on a weekend getaway with people you like to spend quality time with
- Go for a long walk with a friend

## Practise Meditation in Motion

*"Yoga is the journey of the self, through the self, to the self."*
*–The Bhagavad Gita*

There is a reason why so many actors are big fans of yoga. Yoga and acting have much in common. Yoga, like acting, is a practice. Yoga also teaches many skills critical to good acting: body, mind, and spirit connectedness, attention to breath, grounding, body awareness, being present, relaxation, and patience, to name a few.

Although I am not religious, I often refer to yoga as my "church." What is your church? What calms and grounds you? Walking? A long drive? Dancing to your favourite playlist in the middle of your living room?

Whatever your "church" may be, meditation in motion is a powerful tool to recharge and clear the mind, which is probably why it is often referred to as **medication in motion.**

Here are a few guidelines that will grant you maximum benefit:

1. **The activity should require your body to be in continual motion.** Repetitive motion works best. When we are still, we think rather than feel.

2. **Do it solo.** If you bring a friend along, meditation is no longer a part of the experience.

3. **Move mindfully.** Don't allow yourself to check out. Track how your breath moves through your body and how that makes you feel. Mindfulness is key.

4. **When you find your "church," make it a habit.** It doesn't have to be athletic.

Your movement could be something as mundane as cleaning the house, as long as it requires slow, repetitive movement.

**The Bottom Line:**

> Being alone with ourselves in motion gets us out of our heads and into our bodies. It allows us to shift our focus from the external to the internal, so we can slow down and listen inside.

**TRY THIS:**

Take up knitting. Declutter a room in your house or apartment. Get a dopamine hit by digging in the dirt. The important thing is to move and keep moving.

### Woo Yourself

*"When I am...completely myself, entirely alone...or during the night when I cannot sleep, it is on such occasions that my ideas flow best and most abundantly. Whence and how these ideas come, I know not, nor can I force them."*
*—Wolfgang Amadeus Mozart*

Although I highly recommend spending time with family and friends, one thing should take priority over all else—YOU! Meditation in motion is one way to listen internally; courting yourself is another.

When we court someone romantically, we take the time to get to know them. We listen intently to their every word. We go out of our way to plan exciting things to do together. Why? Because we want to win the other person's heart. What about winning your own heart? What about really listening to yourself? What about taking yourself out on an adventurous play date? This isn't a silly idea, nor is it selfish. How much time do we spend getting to know ourselves? Not the selves that we pretend to be—our authentic selves.

Okay, I admit, it sounds a little crazy, but kids get to go on play dates, so why not adults? And isn't that what actors get paid to do—play? Think of it as self-care. Most of us take our cars in for regular maintenance, but what about ourselves? We need maintenance too!

Like meditation in motion, the key to a successful play date is to go it alone—no friends, no special somebody, not even your dog! No distractions of any kind. This is about you. Plan your play date. Something that resonates with the child within. Something that you would enjoy doing but wouldn't typically take the time to do, especially by yourself.

Challenge yourself by stepping outside of your comfort zone. For me, that meant doing *anything* in public by myself. I'm an extreme "E"; I hate being alone, or at least I used to. On my first couple of play dates, I had to remind myself that "No one grows in their comfort zone." Initially, I resisted. I devised a gazillion excuses for why I couldn't. "I'm too busy. I have too much work to do." Finally, I decided to commit to one afternoon, mostly so I could reject this silly idea once and for all.

One of my greatest fears was going to a movie by myself. For all you introverts out there, it's probably no big deal, but for me, it was terrifying! Whenever I went to a movie with friends, I noticed people sitting alone, and I felt sorry for them. "They have no friends…how sad." I didn't want to be one of *those* people! As an extrovert, it never occurred to me that *those* people chose to be alone.

My first play date felt weird, as first dates often do. My creative self and I weren't well acquainted. It also felt self-indulgent. And it was! How dare I take time for myself? And what was with all *those* people going to the movies by themselves anyway? There were so many of them, and they didn't seem sad at all; in fact, they seemed pretty comfortable, happy even.

Seeing a movie by myself was an awakening. I watched and listened in a way I hadn't before. I grew a little that day, and every play date after. I was stepping outside of my comfort zone, and I liked it. I liked it a lot. It made me feel like I had accomplished something big. And who knew I was such good company! That play date was the first of many, many more.

**The Bottom Line:**

Spending time alone on a play date allows us to listen inside.

### TRY THIS:

Compose a list of possible play dates. Choose one. Schedule your play date. Commit to that play date as you would commit to any other priority on your weekly schedule.

*A few ideas to seduce your artist*:

- Spend an afternoon going to garage sales or go thrift-hunting and put together a fun outfit. Give yourself a spending limit.
- Take a creative writing class or workshop.
- Wine and dine yourself at a restaurant you have never been to before.
- Learn a new skill by watching a "how-to" video. How to: change the oil in your car, bake sourdough bread, wallpaper, or build a deck.
- Do a complete day of silence.
- How about a hot cup of tea and trashy novel?
- Make yourself an inspirational playlist.
- Rearrange your furniture.
- Research and dive into a place you have always wanted to visit. Prepare a meal and listen to music that celebrates that country's culture, OR learn the language spoken in your dream trip destination.

Your natural tendency (especially in the beginning) will be to resist. Resist resisting. Unless it's an emergency, don't let anyone rob you of this precious time. Whatever you choose to do, do it mindfully. Pay attention. Your inner artist will have plenty to say.

## Pamper Yourself

Forget for a moment that tired cliché of the starving artist. I hear it all the time. It's simply not true. Just because you are self-employed doesn't mean you will end up homeless or that you will be waiting tables for the rest of your life. Everyone worries about money, especially if you are self-employed. How will I put food in my mouth and a roof over my head? Even if you win a part in a production or you book three days on a film, in the back of your mind you are always wondering if you'll ever work again. All of these concerns are valid. But if you are good at what you do and do what you love, the money part will take care of itself.

How do I know that? Creatives tend to be resourceful. In my late twenties, I decided I wanted to buy a house. So, I became a part of the Artists in Schools program and went up north to teach theatre for a month or two every year until I had enough cash put away for a down payment. Then, I got the itch to travel, so I got myself some roommates. Just because you're an actor doesn't mean you have to live like a pauper; it just means you need to be resourceful!

The truth is, spoiling ourselves is rarely about money. It's more about how we spend the money that we have. Most of us squander money on frivolous things. We're running late for work, so instead of taking the bus, we call an Uber. We hit up Starbucks three or four times a week. (Guilty.) Maybe we go out for lunch three out of five days because we didn't take five minutes to pack one. We order Skip the Dishes because we didn't make it to the grocery store, and even if we did, we're too tired to cook. We subscribe to three streaming services when one would be enough. And how do we manage to scrape together enough money to purchase the latest iPhone? Do we really need one?

It is all the little things that make you broke. The solution is simple. You need to reassess where your money goes and then make some adjustments. Even if you are on a tight budget, there is no need to deny yourself small pleasures.

**The Bottom Line:**

Stop throwing your money away on things that give you little payback. Be as generous to yourself as you are to others.

**TRY THIS:**

> Make a list of five ways you throw away money.

> Make another list of five ways you would nurture your artist self if you had more money.

> For the next month, take the money you would typically spend on wasteful things and indulge in one of the things on your list. A set of really nice sheets? A ticket to a musical that's coming to town? An improv class? Or shoot higher—have a long-term spoil like a trip to the Edinburgh Fringe Festival. (Okay, now I'm projecting my next spoil onto you.)

## Drag Your Ass to Class

There are days when we don't feel up to being in an acting class or rehearsal. If you are puking up a lung or spreading nasty germs, *please* stay home, but if you are having a crappy day (or even a crappy week), show up anyway. Acting can stir up our emotional pot. Sometimes we don't want to deal with those emotions. The trouble is, the longer we stay away, the harder it is to come back. Not showing up can snowball.

That is why I offer my students a "blanket day." One for each term. When a student claims their blanket day, they are only required to show up and observe. Nothing more. No explanation required. No participation required. Some students even bring their favourite blanket from home.

Missing an acting class or rehearsal is not like missing a psych class. You can't borrow someone's notes and catch up. Acting is about doing. About playing. About exploring. And you can't do any of that if you aren't there. When you show up for class or rehearsal, even if you are unable to participate, you are in the room. You are present. You can learn a whole lot by observing the director and the other actors.

## Avoid Multitasking

Multitasking does not work, or should I say it doesn't work well. We check our text messages when we are stopped at a red light, fold our laundry while our best friend shares her recent breakup, take a call while we are out for dinner at a restaurant with our special somebody, and learn lines while watching Netflix. When we do this, one (or both) of the tasks is compromised. We may get the tasks done, but at what cost?

*I am not asking you to question your ability to multitask. I am asking you to question the result.* If you're folding laundry and talking on the phone at the same time, the world isn't going to end, but even then, I question how well you are listening to the person on the other end of that call. When the director is giving actor notes following a run, and you're checking messages on your phone, you are missing out. Even if the note is not for you specifically, you can learn from it. You can learn *what not to do.* In these moments, we may say, "Sorry, I missed that. Can you repeat what you just said?" The reason you missed it is because you are not fully present.

Ask yourself the following questions: When I multitask, can I complete each task in a quality way? You may be able to do two things at once, but if you cannot do either of those tasks well, are you accomplishing what you set out to accomplish? If the quality of "the doing" suffers by 50%, is that success?

As with all rules, there are exceptions. I, for instance, often listen to theme-related music when writing a play. For me, the music inspires rather than distracts. Actors are often called upon to multitask. An actor has to walk and talk; they have to move and remember their blocking or say a line while lighting a cigarette. Musical theatre performers have to sing and dance simultaneously. A musician may have to play an instrument while singing. The difference is that the artist has rehearsed that moment over and over again. Actors also learn their lines from what they do.

**The Bottom Line:**

Sometimes we have no choice but to multitask, but in general (and I hate to be general), we should avoid multitasking whenever possible. We cannot give any of those tasks our full attention when we attempt to do multiple things at once.

## Limit Your Time on Social Media

*"I fear the day technology will surpass our human interaction. The world will have a generation of idiots."—Albert Einstein*

I can hear you groaning; I know, I know, the last thing you want is a lecture on social media from a Boomer. And yes, I am a Boomer. (Barely.) I typed my university papers on a manual typewriter. There was no delete button, so I had to use Wite-Out. There was no spellcheck, so I had to use a dictionary. There was no such thing as Google, so I had to go to the public library to do research. Thank God for advancements in technology!

Unfortunately, those advances came at a price, particularly for actors. When I tell my university students they have to power down until my class is over, the first thing they do is panic. The second thing they do is sweat, like a bunch of drug addicts waiting for their next hit. For the first three or four classes, I know they're barely listening because they're too busy counting down the minutes until they can check their notifications. But they adapt.

Think for a moment how much time you spend on social media. Two or three hours a day? More? Rather than living your own life, you are watching the highlight reel of someone else's. It seems like everyone in the world is living a glamorous, successful, joyful life—everyone but you.

In our tech-savvy world, we spend too much time hyper-focusing on the external. Selfies are a prime example. Snapping a picture of ourselves is about presenting a picture-perfect version of ourselves to the external world. But is that selfie who you are, or is it a picture of how you want the world to see you?

Our phones are designed to engage us and keep on engaging us. Studies indicate that social media leads to loneliness and depression. It reduces our social interaction and detaches us from the real world. It even affects our sleep patterns. But you know all this, so I should probably shut up—but I won't. Overuse of social media can have a devastating impact on your mental health, particularly with anxiety. Although anxiety is nothing new, the level of anxiety I see in my students over the last ten years is over the top. Social media has created an anxious generation. (There is a *New York Times* best seller out right now entitled *Anxious Generation* that is flying off the shelves.) Each year, I spend more and more time talking students down from panic attacks. Let's not normalize that. It can't be fun for the person experiencing it.

Detoxing from social media is tricky. And no wonder. Most of us have our phones on our person 24/7. Even when sleeping, our phones are within arm's reach—just in case. The only time we take a break from our digital fentanyl is when we are forced to. Whenever we have a spare moment, what is the first thing we do? I don't have to answer that one, do I? The more we use social media, it seems, the more we want to use it. That sounds an awful lot like an addiction.

I know what you are thinking: "My relationship with my phone is none of your business, Cairn!" And you would be right. But what if I told you that your love affair with social media is getting in the way of you becoming a better actor? What then?

Don't get me wrong, social media is a great way to connect with others, but if we are constantly competing with strangers for likes, obsessing over how many followers we have, or checking for notifications, our self-esteem is going to take a hit. More importantly, while we are consuming social media, we are not connecting with the real world. We are not listening. And we are not present—all prerequisites for skillful acting.

Think about what you are missing: a shared smile with a stranger, a friendship that might have been, seeing the sadness in the eyes of an unhoused woman on a street corner, uncomfortable moments in an elevator with a stranger.

**The Bottom Line:**

Actors are observers of the human condition. How can you be an observer if you don't look up from your phone? Setting limits on social media and sticking with them will allow your body and mind time to rejuvenate. Your phone needs to recharge, and so do you!

**TRY THIS:**

I implore you to watch the two links below. "Look Up" and "An Update." I am confident that it will inspire you to change your relationship with social media. I know, I'm a Boomer; what do I know? Maybe nothing. Humour me. Be a trier!

https://www.youtube.com/watch?v=Z7dLU6fk9QY

https://www.youtube.com/watch?v=GXc1RhE0gAs

**TRY THIS:**

How long are you awake before checking your phone for messages? For most of us, it is within five minutes of waking up. What would happen if you ignored your devices for the first hour? I promise that the world isn't going to end, although at first, it may feel like it.

**AND THIS:**

During the day, power down for another hour. How did your time without your phone affect you? How did it make you feel? Did you smell things you had never smelled before? Did you see things you hadn't noticed before—maybe the weight of the snow on a tree branch? Did you feel more present? Did you find yourself engaging more with people you don't know? Maybe smiling at a stranger on the street? Meeting eyes with someone you find attractive? Consider this mining for actor gold.

## Listen For Your Call

Every person has a calling—a feeling, a burning desire, an unrelenting voice inside that beckons, a flame that burns. People are called all the time. Trouble is, sometimes we don't hear that call. Fear is a powerful thing. It can be all-consuming. Rather than face our fears, we cover our ears and pretend not to hear them. "La-la-la-la…I can't hear you!" "I'm comfortable where I am, thank you very much!"

I, too, failed to hear my call. My students were always telling me how much they enjoyed my classes, always bugging me to teach more. Although I appreciated their kind words, their words, for the most part, didn't move me to action. Until my phone started ringing. And kept on ringing. It was as if someone was yelling at me: "Hey, Cairn! Wake up! I've been calling and calling. Answer your damn phone!"

Although I had been writing plays and teaching at the university and theatre schools for many years, it never dawned on me to open a theatre school. Was this a call? When I least expected it? At the most inopportune time? I was considering retirement! Over the years, I have received many "calls" and learned that if I am being called, I should answer. And so I did. Eventually. On the precipice of retirement, I decided to open my theatre school.

At first, I tested the waters, offering only two classes. Before I knew it, all my classes had a waiting list. In the second year, I had to hire other teachers. My only regret was not hearing that call twenty years sooner. (It probably wasn't the right time…at least that's what I tell myself.) I'm having the time of my life! No scenes to mark. No lectures to give. The truth is, if I weren't being paid, I probably would show up for work anyway. (Don't tell anyone…it's a bonus to get paid for doing what I love.)

If your phone rings, inviting you to audition, that is a literal and metaphorical call. If someone offers you a part in their short film, that is a call. If you have always wanted to write a play and you bump into a stranger in a coffee shop who happens to mention a playwriting class that is starting next week, that is also a call. If your friends and fellow actors keep telling you that you belong on stage, listen to their call. They see what you already know.

**The Bottom Line:**

Calls happen all the time. Listen for them.

## Synchronicity

*"A meaningful coincidence of two or more events where something other than the probability of chance is involved"—Carl Jung*

Theatre school productions often run on a shoestring budget. My theatre school is no exception. A couple of weeks ago, I announced to my cast that we have a lot of "door-acting" in our upcoming production and would require a sturdy rehearsal door. I followed that up by saying that, unfortunately, the school does not have the funds to build one. They looked sad. That's when I told them to "Have no fear; the Theatre Gods are here." They laughed, of course. I didn't.

I knew that if I put something out in the universe, my call would be answered. And I was right. One of my students happened to be a skilled machinist, he happened to know someone with an old wooden door they were willing to donate. Two weeks later, I was gifted a beautiful steel-framed door that any production manager would be jealous of. (Thank you, Vance!)

Have you ever felt like the universe was trying to tell you something? Like, "Hey you, over here. Keep looking, you're getting warmer..." Some people would call it a coincidence. I call it synchronicity.

**The Bottom Line:**

Go on. Be a trier. What have you got to lose? Put your desire out in the universe. Then wait for the universe to answer.

# ACT III: ACTING THEORY

## Scene i

### STUFF ABOUT STAN: A BEHAVIOURAL APPROACH

### Stanislavski: The System

Who the heck is Stan? When I mention *Stan,* I am referring to the father of modern Western-based acting technique, Konstantin Stanislavski. It would be impossible to discuss contemporary acting theory without throwing his name around a whole lot. Stanislavski was a talented Russian director and actor determined to develop a training system to help actors overcome acting blocks. Stan researched his ideas as a scientist might conduct an experiment. For most of the first half of the twentieth century, the Moscow Art Theatre became his laboratory and his students, his guinea pigs. The fruits of his labour came to be known as ***the Stanislavski System.***

Although many acting theories have been introduced before and since, most modern Western acting theory is rooted in the principles introduced by Stanislavski more than a hundred years ago. To this day, Stan's behavioural approach remains the most popular acting method practised in North America.

### Given Circumstances, or "W4"

*"Who am I? What will I be? Why am I here? Where am I going?"*
*—Stan*

Let's begin our discussion of Stan with one of the key elements of storytelling: given circumstances. *A Practical Handbook for the Actor* (assigned to me in theatre school) defines acting as: "Living truthfully under the imaginary circumstances of a play." Given circumstances are the four "Ws" of theatre. If used effectively, the given circumstances invite the audience into the world of the play—the who, what, where, and when will have a profound effect on how you play out a scene.

Most plays are made up of a series of scenes. The given circumstances of each scene are like pieces of a puzzle; if a piece is missing, your puzzle will be incomplete. For the audience to follow the storyline, most playwrights (depending on the style) will answer the following questions:

When does the story take place?
Who are the characters?
Where are they?
What is going on?

**When.** In every play, we must consider when the story takes place. A play set in the Victorian era will be designed, directed and performed in a much different way than a story that unfolds sometime in the future. Set, costume, lighting, and acting style are all heavily influenced by the period in which our story unfolds.

**Who.** In a play's introduction, we often meet the protagonist and other key characters. We see how each character relates to another. Maybe the characters make up a family or a group of friends, or maybe they are strangers. The actor needs to figure out who they are in relation to the other character(s) in the scene. If it is a two-hander, is the other character my husband, a burglar, or my secret lover? Are they my boss, or a hostage-taker?

Understanding one character's relationship with another is critical because, as my mentor Per Brask often says, "We behave according to who is in the room." You behave differently when you are out with your friends at a party than you would if you were speaking to a two-year-old or a cop who has just pulled you over for speeding.

**Where.** The *where* is incredibly important to the scene and the play as a whole. For instance, master Canadian playwright George F. Walker sets a series of six plays, aptly named *Suburban Motel,* in a run-down seedy motel.

The setting, or *where* of each play, in this case, is very specific—a motel. Why does Walker set six plays in a motel? Why not in someone's apartment or a cottage by the lake? The details are key to understanding the playwright's intent. Playwrights don't just pick given circumstances out of the air. It is our job as actors to ask ourselves questions—a LOT of questions. Like, why a motel rather than a hotel? How does a motel differ from a hotel? Answer: Motels are lower-end and often frequented by people in lower income brackets and for shorter periods. A lot of shady stuff goes down in a motel room: drug deals, prostitution, affairs, sometimes even murder.

We rarely encounter a CEO on a business trip booked into a motel. A motel attracts a specific clientele, one very different from that of a person checking into a five-star hotel. Motel rooms are often small, conveying a feeling of being trapped, like a rat in a cage. There are usually few amenities and dated decor. Strange smells may linger in the air. Setting a play in a motel tells us a whole lot about the characters who inhabit the story and the tone the playwright wishes to set.

**What**. What in the heck is going on? Another term for "what the heck is going on" is *dramatic action*—more on that later. First, we need to discuss objectives.

## Playing an Objective

*"You must be so thoroughly immersed in the given circumstances of the play, then you decide what it is at any given moment that the actor wants."—Stan*

What is an objective? Simply stated, **an objective is what your character wants in a scene or what your character is going on stage to do.** A sexier way to think about it might be what your character desires. Whether you realize it or not, you are playing an objective every moment of every day. It's just so baked-in that we barely notice.

Although we don't like to admit it, we humans are innately self-serving. In acting, as in life, everything we do is to get something we want. You go to the store to pick up a litre of milk. You go out on a date to explore a romantic connection. Would you show up for work if you didn't get paid? You wouldn't bother to get out of bed if you had no reason to. And even if you choose to lie in bed all day, there is always a motivating factor. Maybe you are hiding from the world, maybe you need a break from the insanity that is your life, or maybe you are avoiding human connection.

We are hard-wired to pursue what we want. You are, in fact, playing an objective right now. You are reading this book because you want something. Maybe a test is coming up, you are passionate about acting and hungry to learn (yay), or you just want to impress a classmate with your book smarts. Whatever we do, we are doing it in pursuit of a goal. Even though you are all reading this book, your motivation for reading it will vary.

## Literal Objective and Underlying Desire

There are two layers to every scene objective: the ***literal*** piece and the ***underlying desire***. Desire is rooted in the motivation to pursue your objective—the why behind it all. Think about it. Your literal objective may be to walk an old person across the street, but if we dig a little deeper, maybe you are doing a good deed to feel better about yourself. A defence lawyer's literal objective may be to deliver a summation, but her underlying desire is to convince the jury members of her client's innocence. **Everything that a lawyer does, every word she utters, should be in pursuance of her underlying desire**.

## Be Specific

Hanging front and centre on a wall in my office is an embroidery hoop with this beautifully hand-stitched quotation: "***Generality is the enemy of all art***." It was a gift, lovingly crafted by one of my students. Anyone who has ever been taught by me has heard this phrase ad nauseam. In fact, if I say, "Generality is..." nine times out of ten, my students will chime in with "the enemy of all art." If I had only one quote to offer a developing actor, it would be this one.

Unfortunately, I cannot lay claim to these words. They were uttered long ago (somewhere between 1880 and 1938) by our friend Stan. Since Stanislavski was a legendary Russian director, it is no surprise that he said many mind-blowing things, but none so important as this.

Over the years, I have come to the realization that generality isn't just the enemy of all art—it is the enemy of everything! Would you get on a plane if the pilot told you they would be landing "somewhere" near the landing strip? Specificity is important.

So, what does "*Generality is the enemy of all art*" mean to you as an actor? Basically, it means there is no "sort of" in the art and craft of acting, and there is certainly no room for "sort of" when choosing an objective or playing an action. Put simply: ***Be specific.*** If a director asks you what your character wants and your answer is wishy-washy, it means you will be tentative in playing that objective on stage. And if you don't know what you are going on stage to do, neither will your audience.

If your audience is in the dark, they will lose interest. No, they will not suddenly sit up in their seats and shout, "I have no idea what that actor is doing! I'm outta here!" They just won't find the performance compelling. That is why an actor must commit 100% to what they are doing on stage, 100% of the time.

## One Objective at a Time, Please!

Being specific means you cannot play multiple objectives at once—it muddies the waters. If a playwright has written more than one objective in a scene, it usually means the character's objective has been reached, or abandoned, or they have moved on to pursue something else.

With each scene, your character will have a new objective to play. If the objectives are the same from one scene to the next, the playwright would only need to write one scene. Having said that, just like you have immediate goals, you also have big-picture goals. If you want to be a doctor, you aren't going to achieve it in a day. You'll have to graduate from high school with high marks, then go to university and do the same. Finally, you'll have to write the

MCAT. To pass the MCAT with flying colours, you will have to do a lot of studying.

**The Bottom Line:**

> Characters in a play are just like us; they have short-term goals and long-term goals. Which brings us to a discussion of what good ol' Stan referred to as the ***super-objective.***

### Super-Objective

*The character has to have some arc. The character has to go through an event and be changed by the human event."—Stan*

***A super-objective is a big-picture goal.*** To find the super-objective, you must first consider the play as a whole. Let's review what we have learned so far: We know each character has a scene objective. We also know that the chosen objective will be different for each scene. When we string all the scene objectives together (the character's throughline), those objectives should lead us directly to the super-objective.

Unlike a scene objective, a super-objective is much larger in scope. It encapsulates the character's goal for the entire play, which is why you must read the whole thing before diving into scene analysis. If you don't, the puzzle will be missing pieces, and you need all of those pieces to see the full picture.

**The Bottom Line:**

> Knowing your super-objective will allow you to make informed choices about your scene objectives because they will lead directly to the super-objective.

### Stating Your Objective

Whatever objective you decide to play, phrase it in a way that lights your fire! If you aren't excited about playing your objective, why would an audience be interested in watching you pursue it? First, make sure you use the first person. *I want (fill in the blank).* Second, it must be exciting enough to compel your character to action. Phrasing is important. *Winning back the love of my life* is much more exciting than *Asking out an old boyfriend.*

### Conflicting Objectives

*People don't go to the theatre to watch people get along.* Think about your favourite movie or series. I guarantee the protagonist has an objective that directly conflicts with another character's objective. If Suzie wants to date Becky and Becky wants to date Suzie, there is no conflict; if there is no conflict, there is no dramatic action. Suzie will ask Becky out on a date, and Becky (because they both want the same thing) will say yes—no drama, no scene—or at least not a compelling one.

P.S. With a seasoned playwright, objectives aren't always stated or obvious. Characters may imply what they want, but don't usually come out and say it. And if they do, it usually happens at the play's climax. You may have to get out your shovel and do a little digging.

**TRY THIS:**
Watch your favourite movie or show and track the journey of one of the main characters. What is their objective in each scene? What is their super-objective for the entire movie or episode?

**WARNING:**
Allow me to apologize in advance for robbing you of the pure bliss that comes from simply being an audience member. Once your analytical brain is set in motion, your friends may no longer want to go to the movies with you. Now that you know how dramatic writing works, picking apart every scene or story will become nearly impossible to resist.

### Choose to Care

*"When an actor is completely absorbed by some profoundly moving objective so that he throws his whole being passionately into its execution, he reaches a state we call inspiration." —Stan*

***Always choose to care.*** Choosing to care about what is happening in the scene makes it cook. This does not mean you have to choose to care about the welfare of the other characters in the scene. If you're playing a prisoner of war, for example, you need not care about the welfare of your captor, but you do need to care about escaping from them, even if you are unsuccessful. The desire to escape will drive the action and make it compelling to watch, which brings me to my next point…

## Always Play to Win

Would an athlete train for the Olympics without wanting to win a gold medal? This is highly unlikely, because without motivation and drive, that athlete would never reach that level of excellence. If a person has no desire to win, their chances of winning are slim to none.

We just aren't interested in watching people play to lose. Have you ever had a friend who constantly plays to lose? They say they want a job but never get around to filling out a job application. They say they want a relationship but never leave their apartment. It's kind of soul-sucking to be around that person, right?

We are drawn to motivated characters, even if they are motivated to do horrific things. Take Lady Macbeth, for example; maybe we wouldn't want to be her best friend, but we can't help but be fascinated by her. She is willing to do just about anything to elevate her husband's power and, in turn, her own:

I have given suck, and know
How tender 'tis to love the babe that milks me:
I would, while it was smiling in my face,
Have pluck'd my nipple from his boneless gums,
And dash'd the brains out, had I so sworn as you
Have done to this. —*Macbeth*, Act I, Sc.7

Wow—now that is cold! If you give your word to Lady M, you better follow through! She wants her hubby to murder King Duncan so badly that she claims (and I believe her) she would not only kill but violently kill her child while that beautiful babe suckles contentedly at her breast. She implies that if Macbeth doesn't do the deed, he is clearly weak in comparison. This scene demonstrates the cruel lengths Lady M will go to get what she wants.

Most folks are not interested in watching a character play to lose. The audience (in most cases) wants Lady Macbeth to lose, but her fight for power is pretty darn exciting to watch. If the Big Bad Wolf doesn't want to get inside the houses of the Three Little Piggies, and the piggies don't care if they are served up on a platter for lunch, then who cares? Definitely not the audience.

Fascinating characters want more than anything to be successful in achieving their goal. ***An actor's single motivation must be to complete their task or objective.*** An audience loves to watch the battle to win, even if the character loses. We love cheering on the underdog, especially if they fight like a rabid dog to get what they want. These are the performances we remember long after the curtain falls.

It may also be helpful to ask yourself if the other characters in the scene help you achieve your objective or if they stand in the way of getting what you want. Let's say your character wants to rob a bank, but the other characters in the scene have nothing to do with your objective—more than likely, it will not make sense dramatically. But if the other characters in the scene are conspiring to plan the bank robbery or want to talk your character out of robbing the bank, that would be dramatically interesting.

## Must Be Achievable

Whatever objective you choose, it must be achievable, which means you must be able to begin doing it at any given moment. If Suzie wants to ask Becky on a date, she can start pursuing that goal immediately. The objective should also be achievable within that scene. If Suzie aims to marry Becky, I'm sure she won't be able to pull that off in one scene. Your objective must also be something the character can fail at. If Becky is going to ask Suzie on a date and the audience knows Suzie will say yes, who cares? If your objective is to answer the door, then more than likely, it isn't something you will fail at; therefore, it isn't the most inspired choice.

## Acting in a Vacuum

And don't forget the other characters on stage with you, even if they are minor characters. If you fail to do that, you are acting in a vacuum.

Your character doesn't just need to want something; whatever they want has to involve the other character(s) in the scene. Think about it: If your character wants something that has nothing to do with the other characters on stage with them, why would the playwright bother to include them? They would serve no dramatic purpose. This applies not only to the character you are directly speaking to, but also to the entire ensemble—even if those characters have no dialogue.

## Subtext

Subtext is the underlying meaning beneath a line, what is implied rather than said—the intention behind what we say. *We don't really listen to what people say. We listen to what they mean.*

At first glance, a line may appear to have nothing to do with your objective, but remember, *a playwright rarely has a character come right out and directly state what they want.* The exception might be toward the end of a scene or play when subtext becomes context. If my objective is to be friends with someone, for example, I wouldn't state it. Imagine someone approaching you and saying, "Will you be my best friend?" It doesn't happen… well, maybe if you're five. People usually work up to something or imply rather than state. As actors, we need to "read between the lines."

## Scene Cap

Once it is clear whether you have failed or succeeded in achieving your goal (try as we may, we don't always get what we want), the scene is usually over, or the character moves on to pursue another goal. The success or failure of that objective is often referred to as a *scene cap.*

## Obstacles

Stanislavski referred to the hurdles that get in the way of getting what we want as ***obstacles.*** If, for example, Suzie wants to ask

Becky out on a date but isn't sure if she is gay, that would be an obstacle because it gets in the way of Suzie achieving her goal. If Becky already has a girlfriend, that would be another obstacle. If she can't find a moment alone with Becky to ask her out, we have another. Most of the time, a character takes on one obstacle at a time. The more obstacles the character has to overcome, the more dramatically interesting the scene will be to watch.

## Playing Action

From what we learned at the beginning of this chapter, we know that acting is defined by our friend Stan as *"Taking action within the given circumstances of the play."* We know that the given circumstances are the story's who, what, where, and when (also known as "given circumstances").

We also know that most of the exposition (in traditional dramatic structure) is often revealed in the play's opening moments, giving the audience a reference point from which to follow the story, but what does *taking action* really mean?

As an acting student, I found the term "physical action" confusing. When I think of physical action, I think of jumping jacks, riding a bike, or smoking a cigarette. This kind of action is more stage business or literal action than dramatic action; there is a big difference between the two. Action (in the context Stanislavski was using) refers to dramatic action. *Dramatic action is what happens in a scene or play.*

Remember the cliché: *Actions speak louder than words?* It turns out that it is very accurate, especially in terms of acting theory. If we look at the origins of the word *actor,* it makes sense. *"To act is to set in motion. To drive forward. To do."* If the actor's job is *to do,* then it is critical that you play action from the moment you hit that stage until the moment you leave. You must always be doing something on stage, and whatever that something is, you must do it to pursue a goal or objective. Otherwise, there is no acting going on, only someone standing on stage spitting out lines in a pre-determined manner. Something must be happening from moment to moment to keep the audience engaged.

Students often ask me how they should deliver a line. Your focus should never be on the delivery of a line. To better understand what playing action is about, ***think about what your character is doing rather than what your character is saying.***

Let's review: To act means *"to do."* Acting is doing. When preparing for a role, the actor must find the scene's dramatic action. If you are not doing, you are not acting. "But how do I play action?" you are probably asking yourself. Have no fear; Cairn is here! To play action, we must verb!

## The Art of the I-N-G

*Verbing or actioning* is a tool many actors use to help expand their repertoire of possible actions. In case you don't remember, a verb is an action word—actors love action words. This technique is so commonplace in the acting world that there is an Actor's Thesaurus dedicated solely to that purpose (*ACTIONS* by Marina Caldarone & Maggie Lloyd-Williams, QSM/ Drama, 2004).

*Instead of thinking about how you will say your line, ask yourself what you want to do with the line.* How will you use this line to affect the person you are speaking to? How will this line help you get what you want? What is your intention? Adding "i-n-g" to the end of a word automatically shifts your brain into active mode.

**TRY THIS:**

Let's play with the neutral line of dialogue below and assign a verb to it:

"How's it going?"

Try verbing this line with each of the verbs listed below.

Possible Actions (Verbs):

Flirting
Intimidating
Consoling
Tempting
Bonding

Investigating
Considering
Avoiding
Confronting
Befriending
Seducing

The list of actions above is only a few examples. There are an infinite number of possibilities you can play on any given line. As a playwright, I can assure you that no line is without purpose. When playing action, variety is the spice of life, so don't be afraid to play something unexpected. Just keep in mind that every action you play should ultimately lead you in the direction of what your character wants.

**TRY THIS:**

Think of something you wanted in the past, then write it down in the present tense. I want… (fill in the blank.) Now, write down all the actions you used to try and get what you wanted. Did you beg? (begg-ing) Did you throw a temper tantrum? (throw-ing a temper tantrum) Did you use your charm? (charm-ing) Did you threaten? (threaten-ing) Were you successful in achieving your goal?

If you could go back in time, would you change or add any actions? This exercise proves that most of us are going after something every minute of every day. It demonstrates that most of us move on to another tactic (try and find another way to get what we want) if we fail.

A character will stop pursuing their objective for one of two reasons: Either they achieve their goal or recognize it is unachievable and move on.

## A Different Action for Every Line

*"You'll never see any two good actors approach a role in the same way." —Stan*

Although a character may say the same line twice, it is rare that the playwright intends for the actor to play the same action on both lines.

The number of possible actions you can play on any given line is endless. Having said that, once you consider the given circumstances of the scene, your list of possible actions will shrink substantially. Every line should have a different action, and every line must be in pursuit of your scene objective, either directly or indirectly.

In playwright Debbie Patterson's scene *"Baby Killer Cat Fight" (Generation NeXXt,* Scirocco Drama, pp. 55–61), nurse Jane completely unravels while advising a patient who is finalizing details for her abortion.

JANE: You spoiled little bitch. I have used my body as a human shield to protect—and I will not have you waltzing in here calling what we do baby killing, bullshit "life begins at conception"—

JANET: BUT IT DOES! I CAN FEEL IT.

JANE: *(Beating her.)* SHUT UP SHUT UP SHUT UP. Can you feel this? Hunh? Can you feel this?

JANET: *(Overlapping.)* Stop stop stop.

*JANE stops. Without looking at JANET, she straightens herself up and picks up the clipboard.*

JANE: All right. We'll see you in two weeks.

*JANE leaves.*

Note the punctuation. (See The Importance of Punctuation, Act V, Scene ii.) The playwright is very specific in her intention. The caps suggest a definite intensity, and the lack of punctuation conveys a loss of control. "SHUT UP" and "Stop" are repeated several times with no punctuation. If the playwright wanted all of the "SHUT UPs" and "stops" to be played in the same way, she would have stopped at one. Playwrights use repetition for a reason. We continue to speak because we haven't been successful in getting what we want.

***When we speak, the person hearing the words is not listening to what we say; they are listening for what we mean.*** How often have you had someone respond to what you have said with, "It's not what you said, it's how you said it!" or "It's not what you said, it's what you meant." That is why, if we have ten people playing the part of Lady M, we will more than likely have ten different choices in what that actor chooses to play on any given line.

## Low-Level/High-Level Choices

Some choices are more exciting than others. When actors first learn the verbing technique, they often opt for low-level choices. Avoid making literal choices like:

Talking
Asking
Speaking
Conversing
Stating
Remembering

The litmus test for quality is to ask yourself if your chosen action could fit any scene or line. Talking, for instance, would fit just about every scene and, therefore, is a low-level choice. High-level choices are usually not actions that can apply to any scene. A strong choice is very specific. The audience will check out if you are playing general action or not playing action clearly.

⚠ **WARNING:**

When you first learn to *verb,* you may feel like you are being asked to intellectualize the acting process, and to a certain extent, you would be right. Be patient. The goal in learning to verb is to become so good at it that you can do it off the top of your head. Eventually, verbing will become spontaneous. Instinctively, you will know the difference between "a line read" and playing action.

## Tell the Whole Truth and Nothing but the Truth

I often joke with my students that I mustn't catch them acting. "If I can see you acting," I say, "then you are not acting well." People outside the theatre often think acting is pretending, but it's not; acting is about telling the truth. Acting is about playing action in the moment, not pretending to. In other words, the action must really be happening. For example, you cannot pretend to seduce the other character in the scene; you must actually seduce them. You cannot pretend to intimidate someone; you must actually do it.

There is a brilliant lesson Stanislavski shares in his first book, *An Actor Prepares.*

On the first day of class, the director instructs one of his students to go on stage and find a brooch he has pinned onto the stage curtain. To entertain her fellow students, the student clutches her chest, yells in distress and runs around like the building is on fire. When she finishes her task, she is quite pleased with her "performance," but when the director asks her where the brooch is, she hasn't a clue. Instead of simply looking for the brooch, she spent the entire time "acting" like she was.

The director then offers her a second chance. He tells her the brooch is valuable and will pay for her class tuition, and that without the brooch, she will be unable to continue her training. This time, she mutters in frustration, painstakingly checking every fold in the curtain. This time, her performance doesn't look like a performance, because she is doing something. She is no longer consumed with the need to entertain.

**The Bottom Line:**

> If your focus is on the audience rather than on what you are going on stage to do, it will inevitably lead to what is often called schmacting.

### Less Is More

Overcompensating on stage is a common acting stumbling block. Many Type A, hard-working acting students work overtime because they feel the need to entertain. And why wouldn't they? It makes sense. Usually when we work really hard, we are rewarded.

By working really hard, students are convinced they will be more authentic. They believe if they work hard enough and are dramatic enough it will translate into a strong performance. In reality, working overtime (like the young woman in the brooch story) will inevitably lead to overacting.

**The Bottom Line:**

> Pleasing the audience can never be your focus. Chances are, if you feel like you are working too hard, or your acting teacher or director keeps saying "Less is more," you are probably overcompensating.

The Janitor's Test

I, too, experienced a Stanislavski moment of truth. I was rehearsing a three-minute, quite brutal fight scene for a university show. For safety purposes, the director insisted that my fight partner and I meet with the stage manager daily at lunch to rehearse our fight sequence. During one of our rehearsals, a university student walked by and heard all the commotion. When he entered the theatre and saw what was happening, he frantically summoned security to come and save the girl who was getting "brutally assaulted."

When I shared this story with my director, he said, "Good for you. You passed the janitor's test!" Huh? "Passing the janitor's test" means that if a janitor (or anyone else) comes into the theatre during rehearsal, they will believe what they are seeing is real. That was a profound moment for me. For the first time, I internalized what Stanislavski meant when he talked about the truth of the moment and the importance of going on stage with purpose.

## Tactics

Let's take a few moments to review: In a scene, obstacles will get in the way of what your character wants—no obstacles, no conflict. Your objective (why you get out of bed in the morning… or don't get out of bed in the morning) directly influences how you get what you want (dramatic action). Being the unique and creative beings that you are, every one of you will go about getting what you want in different ways. Herein lies your creativity.

The way we attempt to overcome *obstacles* in pursuance of our goal is called a *tactic. A tactic is the "how" behind your objective.*

Whether you realize it or not, all of you are experienced in using tactics. For example, if you want to borrow your friend's truck on moving day (the objective), you might tell her how fit she looks (complimenting) and ask her if she has been hitting the gym. The action might be complimenting, but the tactic, in this case, might be buttering her up. There are many ways to butter someone up. Maybe you offer to take her to lunch (bribing), run errands, or help her write an overdue essay. All of these strategies fit under the umbrella of buttering up.

When we want something badly, we go after it in a big way, but if we continue to be unsuccessful, we eventually switch gears. We risk a one-note performance if we play the same tactic for the entire scene. For instance, although I love Marilyn Monroe, in most of her movies, she uses the tactic of "seducing." Sadly, the studios hired her to do just that.

She was hired to seduce, and although Marilyn does it very well, I suspect she was capable of playing so much more.

## Real Life vs. Theatre

I must credit my mentor Tom Stroud for teaching me what I am about to share with you. Although we don't want to play one tactic through an entire scene, we also don't want to switch gears too soon. I often use real-life scenarios to make my teaching more relatable, but we must remember that theatre is not real life.

Playing a tactic on stage and playing a tactic in real life are quite different. In real life, most of us avoid conflict. Conflict doesn't *feel nice.* The problem with avoiding conflict is that it is what brings an audience to the theatre in the first place. Conflict is exciting!

And as I have said previously, no one goes to the movies or watches live theatre to see people get along. Why would they? Getting along may be *nice*, but it's boring to watch.

**The Bottom Line:**

> Because we are taught from a young age to avoid or resolve conflict, when we find ourselves on stage, we tend to abandon a tactic just as we get to the juicy bits. Instead of walking toward conflict, we run away from it. Walk through the fire. Follow the arc. Embrace the conflict!

**TRY THIS:**

Right now, I want you to give yourself permission to behave in ways you would not in your personal life. And really, how much fun is that? Part of the joy of acting is that we get to say and do things we don't get to say and do in our personal lives. Rather than resolve the conflict the minute it gets uncomfortable, move towards it.

## Unit Change

***Switching tactics usually constitutes a unit change or a shift in a scene.*** Sometimes, a playwright will write the word "*beat*" in the script to indicate a shift; sometimes, they will leave it to the director's discretion. Another reason for a unit change is a character entering or exiting a scene (also called a French scene).

A unit change may also occur if a character receives new information. An example would be a woman opening a love letter addressed to her husband from another woman. That new information would be the catalyst for a significant scene shift.

## Putting It All Together

*"The life of a character should be an unbroken line of events and emotions, but a play only gives us a few moments on that line—we must create the rest to portray a convincing life." —Stan*

Since most actors are visual thinkers, the diagrams below may help you better understand how dramatic action and objectives work.

## Diagram A: (Scene)

**Action—Action—Action—Action—SCENE OBJECTIVE**
**(Tactic)**

The dashes above represent the dramatic action the character takes in the scene to achieve their goal or objective. Several actions may fit under the umbrella of one tactic.

## Diagram B: (Scene)

**Action/Obstacle—Action/Obstacle—Action/Obstacle—SCENE OBJECTIVE**

An obstacle is something that puts up a roadblock to hinder a character from achieving their goal. If we map out a through line of action for our character for the entire play, it will look something like this:

**Scene Objective—Scene Objective—Scene Objective—SUPER-OBJECTIVE**

Without a throughline of action, we have no character journey. If there is no character journey (the character does not change from the beginning of the play to the end) there is no story to tell. Note: if a play is structured in a non-linear way, the character will not follow a straight line to a super-objective. They may, for example, begin at the end.

## The Magic "As If"

*"When I give a genuine answer to the "if" then I do something. I am living my own personal life. At moments like that, there is no character. Only me." —Stan*

The magic "as if" spotlights engrossment in the imaginary circumstances of the play. The *as if* provides a path to make those circumstances more relatable. I don't know how often I have auditioned for a film or television role, and the casting director says, "Just be yourself." Imagine yourself in the given circumstances. How might *you* respond to what is happening in the scene within the parameters of the role? It is *as if* you are that character in those circumstances.

According to Stanislavski, a character is the marriage of the role, the given circumstances, and you.

**Role + Given Circumstances + You = Character**

If you are playing a sex trade worker, for instance, and one of your customers is threatening your life, how might you feel? How might you respond? I know what you are going to say… "But, Cairn, I have never been a sex trade worker, so how could I possibly know what I would do?" That, my dear friends, is where Stan's magic *as if* comes into play.

Most of us have never been a sex trade worker, but all of us know what it is to feel fear. Fear is a universal emotion. You may have been swimming alone and been caught up in an undertow. How did that feel? How did your body respond? Did your breath pattern change? Our imagination constructs memories and associations all the time. Those associations may be relatable to the given circumstances of your character.

Stan took that idea one step further. He claimed that if the actor is on their game, you and the character you are playing become one. This is where the line between a character and yourself gets blurred. Modern theatre training is moving away from drawing on personal experience and toward the idea that a character is separate from you—a recipe, so to speak, created from scratch.

But how can that be when you are standing on stage, making creative choices based on your training, DNA and lived experience?

Ultimately, a character isn't something that lives exclusively outside of you because it comes from within you. It's you, but not you. Are you confused yet? Hang in there!

As a playwright, for instance, I am often asked if my characters are based on me. Because I have created that character, it stems from my memories, observations, life experiences and associations. Sure, you could say my characters are bits and pieces of me—but they are also bits and pieces of my research, of people I have interviewed, known, observed, read or heard about. My imagination allows me to build on that. Consciously or unconsciously, as artists, we cannot help but bring ourselves to our work—who else would we bring?

But the truth is, you are not a king or queen, a space alien, or a sex trade worker. Your life doesn't fall apart and resolve itself in ninety minutes. You don't meet and fall in love in fifteen minutes (or maybe you do, but it's certainly not typical!). You have probably never been in a shoot-out, and you have no clue what it means to be a woman living in the Victorian era.

How many of you have landed on the moon? My point here is that as actors, we will find ourselves in all sorts of circumstances that we have never experienced.

Still, you are the foundation on which you build a character. You have been cast in a role because of the unique qualities you bring to it. If ten people are auditioning for a role, you may all have the same recipe (the words in the script), but your auditions will be different from one another because every one of you will bring things to that script that are uniquely you. You are the vessel, separate from the character you create. Your life experience and associations are the starting point from which you launch, but your character will not walk and talk like you or say and do things that you do because your character is not you, although, at times, it may feel that way.

**WARNING:**
The *as-if* can be helpful to you, but avoid choosing relatable circumstances that will re-traumatize you or put your mental health in jeopardy. Although it is a tool designed to help you dig deeper, you need to know your emotional limits if you want it to serve you.

## Stakes

*Make sure your relatable circumstances have the same weight as the given circumstances in the scene.* A mistake novice actors make is picking relatable circumstances that do not have the same stakes as the given circumstances in the script. For example, if your character is bedside in a hospital room comforting his dying mother, relating that sense of impending loss to your hamster dying when you were in the fourth grade is not comparable.

## Stereotypes

In the past, I firmly believed that actors should avoid stereotypes and one-dimensional characterizations. It makes sense. After all, not all sex trade workers are created equal. Some are kind and gentle, some tough and hardened, others incredibly intelligent and vulnerable. The spectrum of sex trade workers is as broad and varied as any other roomful of people.

After training in emotional embodiment, however, I have reconsidered my position. Starting with a stereotype can be a great way to begin exploration. That way, you begin the process of character development in your body instead of in your head. Overthinking gets in the way of that. Embodiment is physical, not mental. Just don't get stuck in that stereotype.

Without nuance, you risk a one-note performance. You are building a character, not a caricature. Human beings are complicated, and so are the characters we play.

## What if?

In Stanislavski's *An Actor Prepares,* the director instructs Vanya (an acting student) to walk on stage and close the door. What could be simpler?

Vanya does not just close the door as requested; he slams it for no apparent reason. This is when the director halts the improv and reminds him that ***all action must have a purpose.*** Simply closing the door will result in mechanical acting because it has no purpose.

The director then suggests that a violently insane man, who used to live in the apartment, has escaped the psych ward and is on the other side of the door. He then poses the question: "What would you do?" Instead of focusing on the mechanical task of closing the door, Vanya focuses on the impending danger. He must prevent the man from entering the apartment. This certainly would change how he closes the door and the action to follow. *What if* he closes the door but has no key to lock it? What then?

Maybe he searches for a key or stacks a bunch of furniture against the door to prevent the madman from entering. In any case, closing the door is now engaging to watch because ***the action has a purpose.***

Let's be straight up. The actor knows there is no madman on the other side of the door, just as you know the living room on set for the play you are in is not your actual living room. Stanislavski in no way suggests that actors should try to convince themselves that the imaginary world they are living in is real. He suggests the actor stimulates their imagination by posing a simple question: *What if?* Rather than asking you to believe in a non-reality, he wants you to invite your imagination to a play date. Instead of saying, "There is a madman behind the door," he asks, "***What if*** there is a madman behind the door?" What would *you* do?

*What if* you sneak your boyfriend in through your bedroom window, and your parents are pounding on the door? *What if* you are awaiting an acceptance letter to a prestigious theatre school, and the mail carrier is standing on the other side of the door holding a stack of letters?

When the director initially asks Vanya to shut the door, his action lacks purpose, other than doing what he has been asked to do. *What if* the director told Vanya not just to shut the door but to leave the theatre and never return? Vanya's slamming of the door would then have a purpose. All of a sudden, the action of slamming the door becomes more engaging.

## You Cannot Play Emotion?

*"When you are choosing some bit of action, leave feeling and spiritual content alone. Never seek to be jealous, or to make love, or to suffer, for its own sake. All such feelings are the result of something that has gone before."—Stanislavski*

Stanislavski believed that actors should never seek to play an emotion. "Whaaat? Don't play emotion!" my students say. "But Cairn, emotion is what theatre is all about!" And that would be right! When students hear this quote, they become confused. Let me clear things up.

Stanislavski is NOT saying you cannot have an emotional response; he is saying that an emotional response must come from something that has been done to you, or as he puts it, "*something that has gone before.*"

You do not, for instance, wake up angry (most of us, anyway). Things happen to make us feel angry. Your puppy pees on the couch, your alarm doesn't go off, someone drinks the last bit of milk so there is none left for your morning coffee, someone steals your car, or maybe your girlfriend ghosts you on social media. Having something done to you brings about an emotional response.

**Stuff happens (Action)—You respond (Reaction)**

When most of us think of something as being dramatic, we associate that with emotion, which makes sense since all action stems from emotion. Emotion occurs as a result of action. But if all actions are emotional, a scene is like a cyclical movement from one emotion to the next, with no sense of where it begins or ends. When things are cooking on stage, the actors are playing out a chain reaction of emotion: action-reaction-action-reaction. We no longer know what came first, the chicken or the egg, because ***both our actions and reactions are driven by emotion.***

In our personal lives, we don't plan how to respond emotionally because we have no idea what will happen next. The truth is, we have zero control over what others say and do. The only real control we have lies in how we respond. If your boyfriend is treating you like crap, for example, you can't change that. Only he can. You do, however, have control over how you respond to him. Maybe you ghost him, give him a harsh warning, or decide to tolerate it. (I hope not.) Ultimately, only he can change the way he is treating you.

Do you consider emotion when pursuing a goal in your daily life? If you want to ask someone out, you probably don't think about your emotional response; you focus on *how* you will ask that person out. Are you going to start with small talk, perhaps asking them about their plans for the weekend? Are you going to tell them how nice they look? Or will you rip off the Band-Aid and spit it out? There are hundreds of possibilities.

In theatre, we not only have to think about how we will get what we want, but we also have to score our emotional journey. Charting our emotional arc is part of that process. Herein lies the problem with Stan's claim that an actor shouldn't play emotion. Theatre and life are different. Although we don't plan our emotional reactions in life, we do in theatre. We know what is coming next. You can pretend you don't, but you do. You know the line that follows yours. You know how the scene will end.

Actors spend the rehearsal period playing with possible choices and exploring them. After opening night, the actor's job is to recreate the score, much like a musician or a dancer does.

No two shows will be the same (that is the joy of live performance), but for the most part, the score has been set. The last thing you should be thinking about on stage is objectives, obstacles, or emotions. That work is for rehearsal, not performance.

When we perform, our muscle memory kicks in, and we play out our emotional score moment to moment, with other actors. (See Act III, Scene ii: Standing on the Shoulders of Stan.) We are essentially playing emotion, but not in our heads—in our bodies. The hard part is repeating those choices as if they were happening for the first time. Repeatability is challenging for actors.

Like the actor, the dancer may think about the choreography while learning it in rehearsal, but eventually, the steps become muscle memory. By the time the dancer reaches performance, the steps are in her body. If they are not, the dancer will second-guess every move she makes. Most of us have been to a dance recital where we see beginners or small children use their peripheral vision to sneak a peek at the dancer beside them. That dancer hasn't committed those steps to muscle memory (or maybe they lack the confidence to believe they have). If they had, the dancer would not need to check in with their neighbour. It is the same when an actor is embodying emotion. They no longer have to think about their emotions because they are in their body, not their head.

However, for the audience to buy into the actor's emotional journey, they need to see the ball of yarn unravel; they need to see the source. The emotion can't come out of nowhere, which is what Stanislavski was warning against. The reaction is, of course, emotional, but it still needs to be in response to something that has gone before. Since you have an emotional score, you know what the something will be.

**The Bottom Line:**

> Your emotional score is in your body, not in your head. Rather than thinking about playing emotion, think in terms of embodying emotion. (See Act III, Scene iii: An Emotional Approach to Acting.)

## Emotion Memory

*"The secret to moving the passions in others is to be moved oneself."—Aristotle*

Most professional actors would agree that to deliver an authentic performance, they must live the emotions of their character. Stanislavski believed that actors need to experience emotion rather than play an emotion. We are all familiar with the term "crocodile tears." As a child, I was quite skilled at throwing a temper tantrum in the middle of the grocery store if my mom didn't buy me my favourite ice cream. My tactic was to embarrass my mother into giving me what I wanted—ice cream. Unfortunately, my mother was on to me. I was "acting" sad and upset, yet there was no red nose or tears to back it up. Rather than feeling those emotions, I was "putting them on." This is what Stanislavski meant when he referred to "playing emotion."

To help actors experience authentic emotion, Stanislavski created a technique called ***Emotion Memory.*** This, of all his techniques, was considered the most controversial. It goes something like this: The actor recalls an emotional memory similar to what their character is experiencing in the scene. This, Stan reasoned, would help the performer conjure a genuine emotional state. Let's say the character you are playing is experiencing a significant loss. Maybe you recall having a miscarriage in the early stages of a pregnancy.

The trouble is, when we revisit a dark, emotional place, sometimes we have trouble finding our way back. Our emotions may get away from us. And that's not good. At the time, Stan had no idea how dangerous digging into our past could be. Over time, however, he began to question the safety of emotion memory and ultimately rejected it.

Another issue, as actors soon discovered, is that emotion memory is unreliable. Can an actor repeat that emotional moment every night and with the same intensity?

**TRY THIS:**
Although I don't recommend emotional memory to actors, if you want to explore it, I advise you to create some personal distance. Rather than using your past to fuel emotion, relate to a friend's experience, or recall something you read in a book or heard on the news. If you insist on digging into your past, make it an old, healed wound rather than a fresh one.

## Scene ii

### STUFF AFTER STAN

*"Create your own method. Don't depend slavishly on mine. Make up something that will work for you!" —Konstantin Stanislavski*

Stanislavski's System directly informed the teachings of some of the most influential master teachers of the twentieth century: Lee Strasberg, Stella Adler, Uta Hagen, and Sanford Meisner, to name a few. As representatives of what Stanislavski spent his whole life trying to achieve, Stan's disciples took elements of the system and made it their own.

## Lee Strasberg: *The Method™*

*"Method Acting is what all actors have always done whenever they acted well." —Lee Strasberg*

Strasberg is often referred to as the "Godfather" of Method acting. Although Lee Strasberg had no formal training as an actor, he practised Stanislavski's system and evangelized many of his ideas.

He, too, rejected the old-school notion of a melodramatic style of acting and reinforced the idea that the actor must work from the inside out rather than outside in. In the 1930s, building upon Stan's teachings, Strasberg began to develop his "Method."

In 1951, Strasberg became the artistic director of The Actors Studio in New York City. *The Studio,* as it is affectionately called, was (and still is) most famous for experimenting with and refining Method acting. Like Stanislavski, Strasberg encouraged actors to dig into their past to create an emotional state. However, it wasn't enough to merely recreate an emotion on stage; he wanted the actor to recapture a life-changing event from their past and inject those real-life feelings into an emotionally charged moment on stage. This, he believed, would influence a character's emotional and physical behaviour.

### Sense Memory

Strasberg took the idea of emotion memory one step further by focusing specifically on the sensual details of the actor's emotional memory: what you saw, heard, tasted and touched. If you recall holding your newborn baby for the first time, for instance, you might remember the sound of your baby's cry, the discovery of your baby's tiny little toes, or the feeling of your newborn's delicate skin against your own.

### Affective Memory

In essence, Strasberg stole Stan's idea of *emotion memory* and combined it with *sense memory.* A new term was born: *Affective Memory.* Although many actors found sense memory to be an effective tool, most found the process to be torturous. The Method™ was particularly revolutionary for film actors. Strasberg's theory was embraced by some of the most celebrated actors of the twentieth century: Marlon Brando, James Dean, Marilyn Monroe, and Robert De Niro, to name a few.

### Method Acting on Steroids

Since Strasberg's method was popularized, many actors have taken it to the extreme. Heath Ledger described the Joker as a "psychopathic, mass murdering, schizophrenic clown with zero empathy." To prepare himself for the role, he locked himself in a hotel room for a month and saw no one. Robert De Niro immersed himself in the world of his character Travis Bickle in *Taxi Driver.* He got himself a taxi licence and worked nights for a month driving a cab in NYC. To prepare for his role in *The Machinist,* actor Christian Bale lost sixty-three pounds, dropping his weight to 122 pounds.

All of these extreme examples raise some important questions: Has Method acting gone too far? Has it been normalized? What is real life, and what is acting? Unfortunately, the media continues to romanticize the idea of the tortured actor.

**The Bottom Line:**

> Strasberg's practices revolutionized acting, but many actors felt The Method put their mental health in jeopardy.

### Stella Adler

*"You must get away from the real thing because the real thing will limit your acting and cripple you. To think of your own mother's death each time you want to cry onstage is schizophrenic and sick."—Stella Adler*

In 1934, Stella Adler spent five weeks in Paris studying intensively with Stanislavski. Adler was so transformed by her time with Stan that upon her return to the U.S., she completely rejected the fundamental principle of Strasberg's method. Adler believed that 50% of an actor's job was internal, including imagination, emotion, action, and motivation, and the other 50% was external, including embodiment and voice.

Adler was critical of the idea of delving into your past. She argued that it was both dangerous and unnecessary. The recipe for good acting was a vivid imagination and a willingness to take a deep dive into the given circumstances. If the character you are playing is a woman fighting for the right to vote, for example, the actor's job would be to immerse themselves in every aspect of being a woman and a suffragette in that place and time.

**The Bottom Line:**

> Adler argued that all of the information an actor needs to make choices is right there in the script. If the actor lived truthfully within the given circumstances, authentic emotional responses would happen organically.

### Uta Hagen

*"It's not about losing yourself in a role, it's about finding yourself in a role."—Uta Hagen*

Stealing from Stan, Uta developed a more practical system of acting. Although she believed the actor should still draw on a past memory, Uta Hagen put the emphasis less on emotion and more on the sensual memory of that experience. How do I feel? What sounds do I hear? What did it feel like? Sound like? Smell like? With this technique, the actor should use substitution to relate to the character.

### Uta's Five Basic Elements

**Substitution:** Although substitution is a variation of emotional memory, Uta was more interested in the *sensations* of the actor's lived experience. The actor would combine the sensual awareness of a past experience with the given circumstances of the scene. Am I hot? Do I have a headache? Am I hungry? Sleep deprived? Nauseated?

**Transference:** The actor's job is to find the connection between themselves and the character they are playing.

**Specificity**: Actors will intuitively know what to do on stage if they rehearse with objects that they may find in a specific "where." For example: A kitchen, playground, or courtroom.

**Authenticity**: To motivate genuine action, Hagen encouraged her students to use props, costumes, and set pieces. In rehearsals, she always had a mountain of props and furniture available for the actors to play with. This created a playful rehearsal environment. Kind of like playing dress-up. You choose a costume, define your role (I'm the mummy and you're the daddy) and then create your world with the toys and set pieces available to you. Then you improvise in that world.

**Preparation**: Hagen also encouraged organic habits based on detailed observations of human behaviour. For example, she developed an exercise called "the basic object exercise." The actor would replicate, in detail, a two-minute daily routine. Something mundane that you do every day but aren't mindful of, like getting ready for bed, packing your lunch, or folding laundry. If applied to a scene, that routine task would then be played out authentically.

## Sanford Meisner

Meisner often bragged that he was Strasberg's oldest professional student. Unlike Strasberg, Meisner believed that although lived experience can help create emotional depth, it is not essential. What is essential is the actor's imagination.

## The Three Elements of Meisner Technique

### Emotional Preparation

Meisner claimed that relaxation and concentration are essential to a strong performance. A tense and nervous body blocks an actor's impulses and takes them out of the moment. It's kind of like going out on a first date. If things are going well, and the couple is connecting, they are not thinking about it—they are in it. The second they start thinking about it, the date becomes awkward.

### Improvisation

Focus should be on your partner, relying on instinct to drive the scene. Actors should only react to naturally occurring stimuli. Something must happen in order to provoke and justify a response. Action-reaction.

### Repetition

Repetition is a key component of the Meisner Technique. He developed a step-by-step process of repeating lines to encourage deep listening and to help students sharpen their natural impulses.

**The Bottom Line:**

> An actor should not be looking ahead or behind; they should be in the present. When two actors listen like their lives depend on it, Meisner likened it to watching a ping-pong match. Organic improvising, he believed, inspires authenticity and deep emotional connection.

## Scene iii

### STANDING ON STAN'S SHOULDERS: AN EMOTIONAL APPROACH

*"Actors are athletes of the heart." —Antonin Artaud*

Although Stan's behavioural approach is still the most universally practised acting technique in the Western world, it has limitations. Critics of Stan's approach object to the idea of using "souvenirs" from the past—requiring actors to relive a traumatic event in order to produce an authentic performance. Actors trained in Method acting are also told that they cannot "play emotion," which means they must distance themselves from the emotion itself. And Method acting focuses more on the role than the audience. In theatre, we must consider the patron in the thirtieth row and whether the audience can "read" the emotions the actor is trying to externalize."

Over the last fifty years, there has been a slow but steady movement toward a less heady, more physiological approach. Less thinking, more embodying. Such a change was long overdue. Actors were in desperate need of a safer emotional practice. That practice began with the **BOS Method** and the discovery of the ***Emotional Effector Patterns.***

## What Are Emotional Effector Patterns?

The basic premise behind the *Emotional Effector Patterns* (EEP) is that your body is emotional. Emotion is our first language—before words. The most mind-blowing part of EEP for me was the realization that *the expression of human emotion is universal.* Regardless of your economic status, what country you were born into, your religious affiliation, or how you voted in the last election, you express basic human emotions in much the same way as everyone else in the world. Each of us has a universal emotive body language that is hard-wired from birth. What an epiphany!

Since emotions are the main source of all human communication, the six universal emotional patterns are recognizable to everyone. If an actor learns how to externalize their emotions, the audience (whether they are sitting in the first row or the thirtieth row) will recognize them!

We all express six basic human emotions:

- Anger
- Fear
- Sadness
- Happiness
- Two Kinds of Love: Tenderness & Erotic

There is an Emotional Effector Pattern (EEP) for each emotion. Each pattern has three distinct parts:

- Facial Expression
- Body Posture
- Breath Pattern

All three parts combine to make up an emotional effector pattern. Through training, actors learn to identify what happens in the body, facial expression, and with our breath when we experience any of the above six emotions. Then, the actor trains to mimic those patterns in a very detailed and specific way.

### An Abbreviated History of the Emotional Effector Patterns

The Emotional Effector Patterns (EEP) are the result of a long-term research project developed at the University of Chile in Santiago in the early 1970s by psychologist Susana Bloch, neurophysiologist Guy Santibáñez, and later, theatre director Pedro Orthous.

Together, they developed a system to train actors to reproduce and modulate emotions by learning and mimicking six Emotional Effector Patterns at will. The good news? This method does not rely on past emotional experiences to reproduce emotion. They named this approach the *BOS Method* after the first initial of their last names (Bloch, Orthous & Santibáñez, 1987). A seed was planted that would forever change how actors work with emotion.

### Alba Emoting™

Although the patterns weren't shared widely with theatre artists until the '90s, Alba Emoting had been in experimental use in parts of Europe and South America for decades. In the '90s, Susana Bloch formalized Emotional Effector Patterns training for actors and others and called it *Alba Emoting*. She also incorporated a safe step-out procedure to help actors return to a neutral state after working with emotion. As the Alba approach grew internationally, it maintained the EEP at its core.

Before Bloch introduced these new ways of working with emotion, most Western acting techniques focused on intellectual and imaginative approaches to emotion. The Effector Patterns were a new and exciting way to access emotions physically rather than mentally. Less attention is given to playing action and objectives (putting us in our heads rather than our bodies) and more attention is given to embodiment and breathing patterns.

## The Emotional Body

In 2018, after years of training and teaching the Emotional Effector Patterns, Laura Bond evolved Bloch's ideas, placing more emphasis on deeper physical embodiment and regulation. She also developed a categorization system for EEP, making it easier to teach the patterns. She called this method *the Emotional Body.*

## Emotional Fluency Training for Actors (EFTA)

Building on Bond's advancements, *Emotional Fluency Training for Actors* was developed through research led by my mentor Tom Stroud and others. This training was designed specifically for theatre practitioners.

Emotional Fluency introduces additional tools for safe and balanced practices and focuses on setting up boundaries between the actors and the characters they play. It also delves into the regulation of emotion and safe restorative practices. At its core, EFTA ensures that the actor is in charge of their emotional practice at all times.

The development from the BOS method to Alba Emoting™, Emotional Body®, and finally to Emotional Fluency Training for Actors (EFTA) reflects a progressive refinement of teaching and applying the Emotional Effector Patterns (EEP) for performance.

## How It Works

The actor learns how to induce, authentically express and manage six basic emotions safely: ANGER (aggression, attack, hate); FEAR (anxiety, panic, danger, fight or flight); SADNESS (crying, sorrow, grief, depression); HAPPINESS (laughter, pleasure, joy); TWO KINDS OF LOVE: TENDERNESS (love of parents by offspring, fraternal/paternal love, friendship) and EROTIC (sex, sensuality, lust).

**TRY THIS:**

To witness human emotional patterns in their purest form, go online and watch some babies in action.

**Anger**

**Fear**

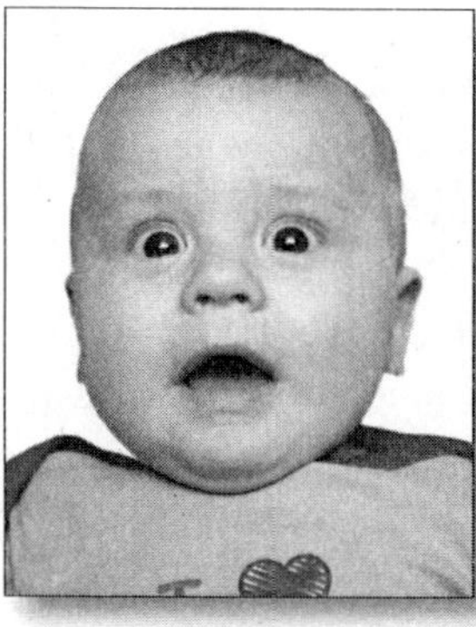

**Sadness**

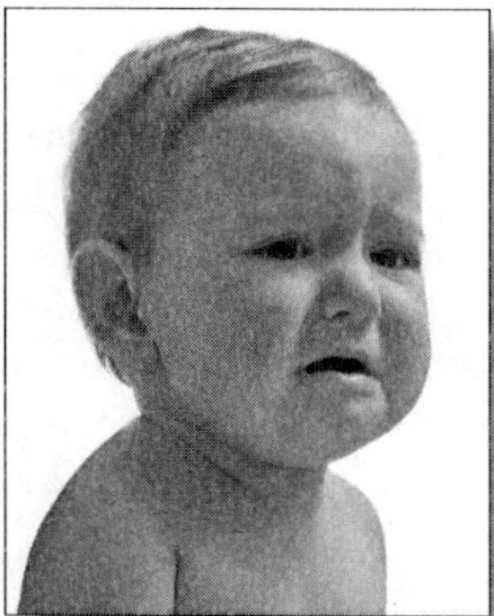

**Happiness**

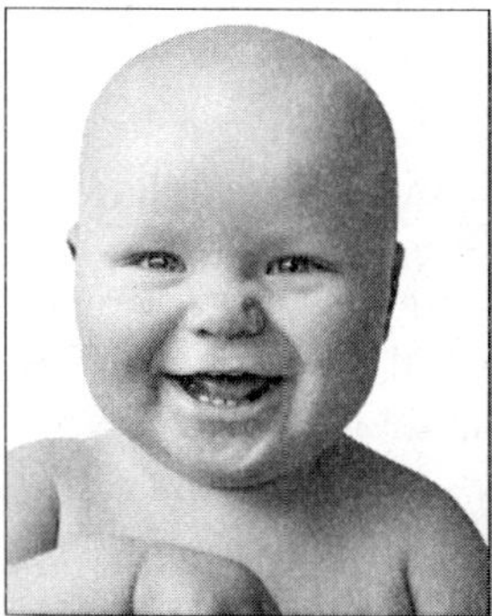

**Tenderness**

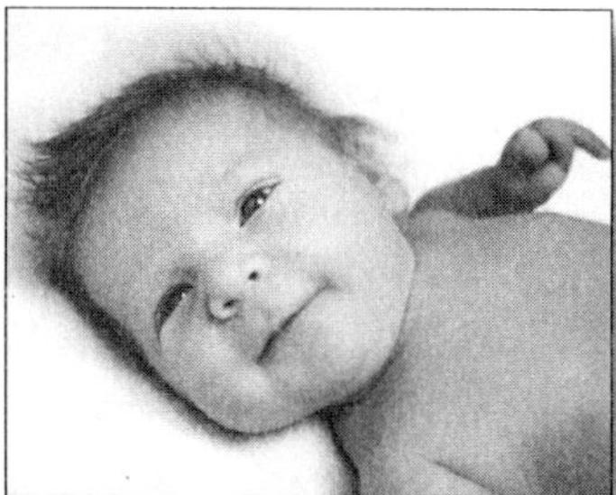

⚠ **WARNING:**

Watching babies is not only immensely entertaining; it's also addictive. Babies are so much fun to watch because they are present and engaged at every moment—eyes open wide, exploring the world, simply responding to stimuli. Babies are tiny emotional athletes. In the blink of an eye, they switch from one emotion to another with 100% commitment. They don't censor their emotion because they don't know how! As we mature, we learn to block or manage our emotions by observing our parents, teachers, friends and siblings.

## The Benefits of the Emotional Effector Patterns

The biggest challenge for an actor has always been taking on the emotional life of whatever characters we play. That means playing a full range of emotions—the good, the bad, and the ugly. We are trained to conjure emotions, not censor them. That's a lot. The question becomes: How do we access all of those "feelies" without compromising our mental health?

Before new ways of working with emotion were introduced, the answer to that question was, "Suck it up, buttercup. It's part of the job!" which may explain why so many actors struggle with anxiety, depression and substance abuse. And although Stanislavski's motivations for developing his system are surprisingly similar to the motivations behind the effector patterns (to help actors live the part truthfully and convincingly night after night), Emotion Memory requires the actor to relive a past memory to get there. (Note: emotion memory is only one small component of Stan's system.) No matter the technique, accessing emotion shouldn't be an occupational hazard.

That is not the case with Emotional Effector Patterns because the training teaches the actor how to enter and exit emotion in a safe and controlled way. You begin and end with a step-in and step-out process, sometimes referred to as the seventh Effector Pattern. There is both stimulation and regulation of emotion. When the scene is over, you can shake off the emotion and return to emotional neutrality—the calm state you began with.

Emotional neutrality is critical to the BOS Method. It allows the actor to create a safe foundation for emotional work in an acting class, rehearsal, on stage or on camera. And, since you are following an emotional pattern rather than, say, reliving a past traumatic experience, you can let go and leave that emotion on stage where it belongs!

If you are in a scene that contains domestic violence, for instance, and you have experienced domestic violence or grew up in a home where that was prevalent, this can be triggering. If you transfer those feelings into a scene, you are no longer the captain of your emotional ship. You may also lose control in a way not intended in the scene. Perhaps you become so emotionally triggered that you cannot put on the brakes. And even if you can put on the brakes, fully living those emotions every time you do a show will eventually take a toll on you.

One of the bonuses of the effector patterns is that you will be using minimal personal experience, which will help you establish boundaries between yourself and the character. You can also stop and start an emotional pattern at any time. The actor, then, is in complete control of their emotions.

Another bonus of the effector patterns is that they are repeatable. (I prefer to use the word *recreate* rather than *repeat*.) The actor can *recreate* that emotion over and over again, and it will lead to the same result. Once the show is up or the camera is rolling, that actor can repeat it night after night or take after take. This means that after show number ten, you will still be able to go on stage and recreate what you did on opening night with the same intensity. You will have a physiological map to follow that will get you there and a step-out ritual that will allow you to wipe the slate clean.

The same cannot be said for Stan's emotion memory. If you are relying on a past emotional experience to get you to an emotional place in the present, is it reliable? Will you always be able to get there? If the answer is "No," that means your character's emotional journey will not be consistent.

The Emotional Effector Patterns also allow the actor to be more connected and present with other actors on stage. Instead of being preoccupied with forcing emotion, you will follow the pattern, and the emotion will manifest itself.

Yet another benefit is that actors can tap into emotions they have repressed in the past. Our childhood experiences shape our emotions. For example, maybe as a child, you were told, "Big girls don't cry," or that anger "isn't nice," and over time, you learned to block those emotions. The emotional patterns allow you to unlock that door and reclaim those emotions in a safe and healthy way.

Once you have a solid grasp of the patterns, you can mix them. It's like knowing your primary colours and then mixing them to create new ones. Red and white mixed create pink. Similarly, shame may be a mixture of sadness and anger.

With experience, an actor can learn to regulate emotions by adjusting the volume up or down. It's like having a remote control for your emotions! Maybe your monologue requires anger at a 9 out of 10 in one moment and sadness at a 5 in another.

## My Personal Experience With EEP

I have to admit that when I first started learning the Effector Patterns, I was skeptical. I certainly wasn't convinced that they were repeatable—it sounded too easy. I also didn't buy into separating myself from the character. Initially, I had to adopt the "fake it till you make it" strategy. And it worked! The more I practised the small details of each pattern, the easier it became.

I also doubted I could authentically feel all those emotions without being personally invested. I had so many questions. If I were super sad in a scene, would it be believable? Would I have a red nose, tears streaming down my face, or a snotty nose without being personally invested? When I first challenged Tom Stroud about personal investment in emotions, he would say, "You only need a little drop of you in there." And he was right! After becoming a believer, I was gobsmacked that all actors weren't being trained in EEP.

Soon after my training with EEP began, I realized my previous training had some serious limitations! Actors like me, trained in twentieth-century methods, were taught to act mainly from the neck up—and that's a problem! A big problem! I was confounded by how much I had underestimated an actor's ability to communicate emotion with their entire body.

Most experts agree that 70–93% of all human communication is nonverbal. Human beings are, after all, animated creatures. Upon this discovery, I had an epiphany: If we are always communicating emotion, that would mean to create complex and layered characters, an actor would need to communicate not only from the neck up, but from the top of our heads to the tips of our toes! Especially if we want the audience to read our "feelies." We must keep in mind that although our brains are essential to good acting, *emotions are physical, not mental.* The body and the mind are not separate. What we feel manifests in the body. We don't think—we emote.

**TRY THIS:**

If you want to see the power of the emotional body, mute the sound while watching a movie with your favourite actor. If the actor is any good, you should be able to follow their emotional journey without hearing what they say.

Although I have only been working with the Effector Patterns for a couple of years, the training in emotional fluency has been exhilarating! I am both excited and inspired by this new way of working. Throughout my career, I have had my share of acting epiphanies, but none like this. Emotional Effector Patterns are a game-changer!

The bad news is that I can't teach you the patterns in this book. First, I'm not qualified to do that (I'm working on it). And even if I were, I wouldn't teach them to you because, as an experienced acting teacher, I believe wholeheartedly in the 3 D's: (1) Discuss, (2) Demonstrate, (3) Do. But even though I cannot teach you the Effector patterns, there are people out there who can. Seek them out!

With permission from my master teachers, Tom Stroud and his accomplice from the University of Toronto, Ines Buchli, and their mentor, Laura Bond (author of *The Emotional Body* and *TEAM for Actors),* I have included some links below. As in all things theatre, the best way to learn the patterns is to do them.

emotionalfluencyproject.com
www.emotionalbodymethod.com

Look for EEP or Emotional Fluency workshops near you. You would be surprised at the number of theatre schools and university programs offering emotional training.

If you wish to find out more, check out the Emotional Body® courses at https://emotionalbody.co/.

If you are interested in learning more about EEP, be sure to work with a certified practitioner. Working with emotion is risky business, and if you don't have an expert by your side to ensure your emotional safety, you may get yourself in trouble. It is best to learn in a workshop setting, an intensive or a weekly class. It is safer, and you will pick up the patterns much faster. I was rather shocked at how easy it was to learn the patterns. Mastering them, however, requires a good deal of practice.

P.S. Just because I believe strongly that this way of training is where the study of acting is headed does not mean I recommend cancelling Stan or any of his disciples. I think Stan's system is a fabulous introduction to acting and scene analysis. He was the dude who started it all!

As Isaac Newton once said, ***"If I have seen further [than others], it is by standing on the shoulders of giants."*** Let's not forget that! Still, we need to build upon what came before and constantly seek out more effective ways of working.

Besides, acting theory isn't all or nothing; the effector patterns can be integrated with any of the acting techniques discussed in this book. EEP is meant to supplement and strengthen existing practice, not replace it.

I want to clarify that the acting theory discussed in this book mainly addresses Western-based modern acting. There are many more techniques out there than I can cover in this book. Explore them all! The more tools you have in your toolbox, the better. When it comes to acting theory, one size does not fit all. No one approach is going to give you everything.

Like most theories, they change and improve over time. As time marches on, master teachers like Laura Bond, Tom Stroud and Ines Buchli will continue to explore and modify techniques so we can learn more effective ways of training. Inevitably, one acting theory will speak to you more powerfully than another. Most will appeal to you in some way.

Take what works for you and leave the rest. What I do encourage in a big way is that you be a full-on trier of everything offered to you before writing anything off. Only then will you know what works best for you.

**The Bottom Line:**

> Actors need to access a full range of emotions. We need to be able to control them while remaining authentic and present. Those emotions also need to be repeatable. If the effector patterns and step-out process are learned and practised correctly, the actor cannot only induce and step out of that emotion at will, but they can also become an emotional athlete.

## ACT IV: ACTING ESSENTIALS

### Scene i

### GROUNDING

In theatre school, *grounding* was a buzzword I heard often but didn't fully understand. What does grounding even mean? In the simplest of terms, grounding is about getting out of your head and into your body. It's about body awareness. It's about being present in the here and now. But how do we do that? We start with the ground, just as the term suggests.

### •> TRY THIS:

Step 1: Remove your socks and shoes. You will feel more confident just by feeling your naked feet on the floor. By connecting with the earth. Think of each foot as a "V": the big toe and pinky toe at the top of the V and the heel at the bottom. Rock forward and back until you find your centre of gravity.

Step 2: Stand with your legs parallel, shoulder-width apart. Your chest is proud, and your chin is tucked in to elongate your neck. Stand tall as if a string is attached to the crown of your head, pulling you upward. When your feet and bones are stacked in this way, you can relax and let go of any tension. Your bones should feel like pillars supporting your whole body.

Step 3: Your knees are slightly bent. If your knees are locked, you will look and feel stiff. Place your hands at your sides with your palms open, facing out.

Step 4: Your eye line is not up or down. Look to the horizon. Eyes are present and alive.

Step 5: Breathe deeply. As Laura Bond says, "Where attention goes energy flows." Breathe into areas of the body where you feel tension. This will also help you feel more present. Avoid raising your shoulders (chest breathing); instead, expand and contract your diaphragm.

If you become distracted, bring your focus back to your breath.

When our feet are rooted and our bodies aligned, we can relax downward to the ground. This is what I call a neutral body. Not the social body you inhabit at a party on a Friday night, but a blank slate in which to build a character.

**WARNING:**
Do not equate a "relaxed body" with a collapsed body. Your body should feel awake and aware, not limp or stiff. With practice, you will begin to feel connected to your surroundings. It is this connection that will keep you present.

Once you feel grounded and relaxed in stillness, take your grounded body for a walk. Ensure that you walk through your entire foot: Heel, ball, toe. Heel, ball, toe. Scan your body. How does grounding affect you? Do you feel more confident? Taller? More aware?

Grounding can be challenging because most of us are disconnected from our neck down. Fear not. We all enter this world optimally aligned and grounded; then stuff happens to mess it all up—If you don't believe me, watch a baby in action. A toddler can sit up tall on the floor with zero effort for hours. When toddlers learn to walk, their feet are pointed slightly inward to help with balance. With every step, the baby's foot hits the floor like a suction cup.

**The Bottom Line:**

If you are still not feeling grounded, no worries! You can learn. How do I know that?—because, at one time, you were perfectly grounded. Not only is it in you, but it comes naturally to you. To be consistently grounded under pressure, however, takes practice and self-awareness, and not just when you are in an acting class—all the time. Practise full body awareness until it becomes a habit.

**TRY THIS:**
The next time you need to have a difficult conversation with someone, or you have an audition, take a moment to ground yourself. Connect with your breath and feel both feet rooted to the ground like a big ol' oak tree. Avoid shifting your weight or shuffling your feet.

You can practise grounding anywhere, anytime: While waiting at a bus stop, at the grocery store checkout, or even on a blind date. Once you get the hang of it, the benefit will be immediate. When our bodies are relaxed and grounded, people sit up and take notice, both on stage and off.

## Scene ii

### LISTEN LIKE YOUR LIFE DEPENDS ON IT

*"When people talk, listen completely. Most people never listen."*
*—Ernest Hemingway*

The most critical skill in acting is *listening*, that's right, listening. Newbies are often surprised by this. Which is why I often do listening exercises with my university students. For instance, I may ask them to pair up and share a personal story with their partner. Once both have had their turn, I ask them to share with the class their *partner's* story rather than their own. That's when the panic sets in. It becomes abundantly clear that most students have done a stellar job of telling their own story, but a pretty lousy job of listening to someone else's. This exercise amplifies how poorly we listen and exposes the naturally good listeners, which, by the way, are few.

The truth is, most of us suck at listening. We would much rather talk about ourselves than listen to what someone else has to say.

When we share a story, the listener is, more often than not, waiting for an opportunity to jump in and tell their own story. The listener may tune in and out, catching bits and pieces, smiling and nodding their heads as if they are hanging on our every word.

Listening, really listening, is difficult. A small percentage of us are naturally good listeners, but for most of us, it is a skill we must learn or, at the very least, improve upon. The best actors aren't just good listeners; they're expert listeners. Don't panic. Just because you're not a great listener does not mean you can't become one.

Actors need to ***actively listen*** all the time. A common mistake beginner actors make is to "act" on their lines and shut down when another character is speaking. Students often ask me what they should be doing when they don't have dialogue—listening, of course! How can you react if you aren't listening? When you are present for only your dialogue, you rob yourself of an authentic reaction. ***The actor's job is to listen and respond, not just respond.***

A good scene is a lot like a pro tennis match. There is a continuous chain of actions and reactions. I hit the ball (the action), and it flies in the air, crossing over the net to the other side; my opponent tracks the ball and finally attempts to hit it back in response (reaction). If that actor on the other side of the net is not "listening," then they will miss the ball, which means they cannot hit it back, breaking our continuous chain of action/reaction.

Without listening, it is virtually impossible to connect with your scene partner and have an authentic reaction. The actor must be listening—and not just with their ears. They must listen with their entire being, like an animal in the forest about to become someone's lunch. If a rabbit is being hunted, that rabbit is not only listening with his adorable bunny ears; he is listening with every fibre of his furry little being. Most people aren't used to listening in this way because, unlike wild animals, we don't live in a constant state of fight or flight. An animal in the forest is used to listening in this way because their survival depends on it. And for actors, (most days) it does not.

Women tend to relate to this kind of deep listening more than men because our safety often depends on it. As women, we are regularly called upon to use our animal instincts. Allow me to set the stage: You're a female living in a large city, it's two in the morning, and you're walking downtown on your way to a bus stop. You're alone. Without looking behind you, you sense someone is following you. Your breath changes, and your heartbeat becomes so loud that you worry the person following you might hear it. Because you are potential prey, you listen to your potential predator not only with your ears but with your entire body, just like that bunny in the forest.

The good news is that although modern life has seriously diminished our ability to listen fully, the potential to listen with animal intensity is alive and well. It's just taking a nap. All you have to do is wake it up! Like the woman walking alone on a dark and deserted street in the middle of the night, you can learn how to listen as if your life depends on it.

⚠ **WARNING:**

Although listening is about connection, active listening does not necessarily mean looking the other person in the eye.

Maybe you are playing an overworked police chief buried in her work. The chief's priority may be to get her job done, and constant interruption would hinder achieving that goal. In the latter case, the chief may not even acknowledge someone entering her office. Maybe the chief wants to convey that she is far too busy for idle chit-chat. For the chief to give her undivided attention, something urgent needs to happen. Still, the police chief is listening—but she is listening for meaning.

How you enter the police chief's office tells them a lot about why you are there. Are you interrupting because there has just been a school shooting, or do you want to invite her to join you for lunch? We are constantly "reading the room" by listening to a person's body language, the depth of their breath, and the intensity and rhythm of their words. ***We are listening to what people mean, not what they say.***

## Scene iii

### BE AT ONE WITH YOUR BREATH

*"When you own your breath, nobody can steal your peace."*
*—Author Unknown*

If listening is the most important skill you can learn as an actor, connecting with your breath is a very close second. What you may not know is that your breath has a whole lot to do with connectedness. Your breath is your superpower! I'm not kidding. Breath awareness will allow you to calm yourself anywhere, anytime—when you address a room full of strangers or are about to walk into your next audition.

As we all know, breath is essential to life, but I want you to go beyond the breathing you do naturally and learn how to control and connect with your breath.

This new skill will take your acting to another level, allowing you to listen more fully. Allowing you to feel more present. Once you do that, you can forget about what's going on on the smart side of the stage (the audience) and focus instead on what's going on between you and your scene partner(s.)

**The Bottom Line:**

Breathing deeply calms your central nervous system and signals the rest of your body to chill out.

**TRY THIS:**

The next time you feel anxious or your nerves get the better of you, ground yourself and then stop and focus on your breath.

Find a comfortable spot in your home with as few distractions as possible. Lie down on the floor and spread out your hands and legs as if you were making a snow angel. Allow your feet to relax and fall to the side. In yoga, this final resting pose is called *shavasana* or corpse pose. (It's hard to get more restful than that!)

> Practise stillness and focus only on the ebb and flow of your breath moving through your body like waves in the ocean at high tide: Inhale through your nose and exhale through your mouth. Allow your breath to travel from your belly to your ribs and then to your chest. Then chest, ribs, belly. If your mind starts to wander (and it will), gently guide it back to your breath.
>
> Another way to quickly calm yourself is to inhale for four counts, hold for four counts, exhale for four counts, hold for four counts, and so on. Repeat until you feel a calmness wash over you.

If you practise connecting with your breath whenever you are stressed, you will learn how to calm yourself. And you don't need to sign up for a yoga class or check out that monk's meditation channel to learn how to do it!

When we connect with someone in a profound way, we may feel as though we are sharing breath. My journey with breath connectedness was the most powerful experience I have ever had as an actor. It was also vital to unlocking an emotional door. Turns out, my emotions were always there waiting to be expressed, I just had no idea how to access them.

Once I learned how to do that, I was able to really hear the words being spoken to me, absorb those words and then respond. With zero effort, I was *feeling* the words rather than pretending I was. For the first time, I understood what teachers and directors meant when they blathered on about organic acting. I was so profoundly affected by breath connectedness that, to this day, it is at the core of everything I teach.

## Scene iv

### BREATHING TECHNIQUE

⚠ **WARNING:**

What I am about to say may shock you.

The first step in discovering the power of your breath is to keep your mouth slightly open at all times. What? I know, I know, it sounds pretty crazy, doesn't it? I had the same response when one of my mentors said this to me the first time. "Seriously?" I thought, "You want me to walk around 24/7 with my mouth hanging open?" The answer is yes. Yes, I do! No, your mouth doesn't have to be open wide enough to drive a truck through it; just slightly open so your breath can move effortlessly. No doubt, this will take some getting used to, but once you know how, being *tight-lipped* will feel alien to you. I bet you're closing your mouth in protest right now!

Most people resist this teaching, and with good reason. First, it feels extremely vulnerable.

Second, we can all recall some well-intentioned adult chastising us for having our mouths hanging open. In the acting world, having your mouth open is cause for celebration because when your breath is allowed to travel freely, your body begins to open up and relax, enabling you to listen fully and completely.

**TRY THIS:**

If you don't believe me, closely observe your favourite actors at work. Unless they are playing a character that is emotionally shut down or angry, most of the time, their mouth will be open, particularly in the most vulnerable moments.

Think for a moment of a child listening to a bedtime story. If the storyteller has talent, that child's mouth will open like a drawbridge, hanging onto the storyteller's every word. The child's breath will become shallow in anticipation of what is to come. When an audience member (for any event) is spellbound, the same thing happens—their mouth

> spontaneously opens, welcoming a magical exchange of breath between performer and audience.

Answer me this: when you cry (that very ugly cry no one gets to see because you only do it alone in your bedroom), can you do it with your mouth closed? Alternately, when you laugh (deep belly laugh, tears streaming down your cheeks, face and tummy hurts from laughing so hard), can you do it with your mouth closed?

No, Cairn, of course I can't! Allow me to offer up my famous bathtub analogy for further clarification: If you want to have a bath, you put a plug in the bathtub before filling it with water to prevent the water from draining out, right? An actor also needs to fill up the tub with water (emotion) but then needs to pull the plug to allow those emotions to run free.

Think about it. When a baby cries, what does the mother do to shut it down? She puts a plug in the baby's mouth! Since the baby can't talk, their only means of communication is crying.

To wail in the way a baby needs to wail, that baby needs to get that pacifier out of their mouth, which is probably why babies are constantly spitting out their pacifiers. That poor baby is seeking emotional freedom. Just like that baby, you need to lose the pacifier (by opening your mouth) so you can freely access emotion.

The scenario where I see actors fail to connect with their breath most often is in auditions, which makes perfect sense. Auditioning can be very intimidating. (It will get easier with time. I promise.) When we are nervous, our instinct is to panic. We take a big, anxious breath and hold onto it for dear life, when we should be doing the opposite. Holding your breath makes your body stiff and rigid, and let's face it, it's kind of hard to kill an audition when you are holding your breath!

The other thing I see all the time is actors chest-breathing instead of allowing their breath to travel deep into the diaphragm, where our emotions live. When you do this, you are bottling up all that tension and anxiety and shutting yourself down emotionally. It paralyzes you. What is the first thing someone says in a tense situation? "Calm down. Take a breath," which is pretty sound advice. The RX for nerves and anxiety is breathing. We would have fewer panic attacks, a lot less anxiety and fewer incidents of road rage if we all learned how to connect with our breath.

The exception to the rule is when we are playing a character who is fearful. When we are in a state of fear or panic, we often hold our breath or chest-breathe.

**The Bottom Line:**

The magical power behind keeping your mouth open and sharing your breath is that it gifts you the ability to listen in an extraordinary way.

**TRY THIS:**

The next time you're having coffee with your BFF, observe. When you are speaking, is your friend's mouth open or closed? When they finish speaking, do they immediately close their mouth? If they do (and most people do), you should probably end the friendship immediately—just kidding! Just because your BFF's mouth isn't open does not mean they are not listening to you at all; it just means they aren't listening fully. I promise, if you start sharing some juicy gossip, their mouth will open. If it's really juicy, their jaw will literally drop.

**AND THIS:**

Now that you know your BFF isn't listening quite as intently as you thought (sorry about that), it's time to check in on your listening skills. When your BFF is talking, is your mouth open or closed? Are you closing your mouth as soon as you have finished talking? If you are, you need to take your listening skills to the gym and give them a solid workout, not just once in a while, but every day. But have no fear. You are not an anomaly. As I pointed out earlier, most of us are better talkers than we are listeners. The good news is that with practice, we can improve our listening skills in short order.

But why is connecting with our breath so important? When actors are not listening fully, the words being communicated do not hit them in the same way. What kind of listener are you? Do you *really* listen to other people? It's a scary process. Deep listening requires immense courage. The expression I like to use to describe it is "opening to be wounded." It sounds terrifying, doesn't it? It kind of is.

Most of us aren't used to this kind of connection, not even with the people closest to us, so if your listening skills suck, your first instinct is going to be to shut down. Don't! You will be astounded and maybe even a little frightened at how vulnerable you may feel. The first time I connected with my breath, I cried—no, I sobbed—like a baby. It was scary as hell, but it was also unbelievably liberating.

When we close our mouths, it is similar to crossing our arms across our chest, putting our hands in our pockets or avoiding eye contact. It's our way of protecting ourselves. We want to keep people at a distance, so they can't hurt us. When we hide in this way, we are also closing ourselves off physically and emotionally. At its very core, acting is about vulnerability. Your breath is the easiest pathway to vulnerability.

**AND THIS:**
Take a moment right now to consider the ways you may hide away emotionally.

## Scene v

### BE IN THE MOMENT

*"If you are depressed you are living in the past.*
*If you are anxious you are living in the future.*
*If you are at peace you are living in the present." — Lao Tzu*

Grounding, listening, and breath connectedness all go hand in hand. So does being present. When we cannot take our eyes off someone, we say that person has "presence." Whether it is someone at a podium speaking to a large crowd, or someone entering a room, we all know presence when we see it. If there are thirty people in the same room, it is the person with presence that we are compelled to watch. But why? We are drawn to that person because they are not in the past or the future—they are present in the here and now. In actor-speak, this is often referred to as ***being in the moment.***

I know, I know, thanks for the life lesson, Cairn, but what does being in the moment have to do with acting? As it turns out, a whole lot. To act well, you must learn how to be present. You are not going on stage to repeat what you did in the rehearsal hall or your performance in a show the night before (what some actors call "phoning it in"). Sure, you have the same lines and blocking, but ***your job is to recreate rather than repeat the moments you have rehearsed.***

The caveat is that being in the moment ain't easy. If it were, Buddhist monks wouldn't spend a lifetime learning how to do it.

As actors, sometimes our nerves get the better of us, and as a result, we start second-guessing ourselves. Am I ready for this audition? Do I know my lines? (Trust me when I say, I've been there.) Our confidence starts to dip, which leads to hyper-self-awareness. Suddenly, we feel as if we are outside of our own body, watching a movie we are in. In an attempt to save ourselves, we may think ahead to our next line (which usually results in forgetting it) or we rewind to a moment two pages back where we messed up a line. We are no longer in the moment. We are somewhere in the future or the past.

One way to hone your skills to be more present is to be curious, like a baby exploring for the first time. Focus on the actors on stage with you. Be hyper-aware of your surroundings. Use all of your senses. Be intensely interested in what you see, touch, smell, and hear. When you concentrate fully on the moment you are in, you will become so engaged with what is happening in real time that you will forget all about what's coming next. Your self-consciousness will melt away.

**The Bottom Line:**

> As actors we need to be somatically aware on stage in a way rarely required in our day-to-day lives.

**TRY THIS:**

To practise being in the moment, let's practise mindful breathing. When you inhale, say: "I am breathing in." When you exhale, say: "I am breathing out." This will occupy your mind so that you aren't tempted to think about all those lines you have to learn or what you are going to wear tomorrow. Mantras keep us out of our heads.

**AND THIS:**

Choose a food that you love to eat, like a bowl of your favourite ice cream or a ripe juicy peach. First, hold the food in your hand in front of you. Look at it with deep curiosity, as if you have never seen that food before. What colour is it? What shape? Touch it. Is it hard? Soft? Cold? Hot? Smell it. Does it have a scent? What does it smell like?

Open your mouth and bring your treat to your lips. Ever so slowly, take a little taste. What is the texture like? Remember our purpose here is to be mindful, so as you take another bite, chew or swallow slowly, luxuriating in each bite. What sound do you make as you chew or swallow? Is it crunchy? Does it make you want to lick your lips? Does the pleasure of eating it inspire vocalization? Go for it! No words, just sounds. "MMmmmm." You may eat the rest of your treat, but do so with painstaking mindfulness, as if you are eating in slow motion. As if this is the most delicious thing you have ever tasted in your life. That is what it means to be in the moment. Details. Using all of your senses. Child-like curiosity.

**AND THIS:**

You're ready to play on the A-Team. I now challenge you to make your favourite meal. Set the table with the best dishes you have. Set out a linen napkin. Eat your entire meal with mindfulness. Your complete focus and enjoyment on your meal, down to each little bite. Don't forget dessert!

Now take that same mindfulness with you on stage. Notice the curl in your scene partner's hair. The softness of their skin as your hand brushes against theirs. The tone of their voice.

## Scene vi

### THE ACTOR IN MOTION

When students first start acting, they have a hard time staying still. When we feel insecure on stage, we do one of three things: close off our body by crossing our arms across our chests (protecting our hearts), putting our hands in our pockets, or overcompensating with unnecessary movement. Or sometimes, developing actors pace back and forth on stage for no apparent reason. When actors feel anxious, they tend to work overtime with their bodies.

To be clear, there is nothing wrong with movement on stage; it becomes an issue when you move unnecessarily because *you* are nervous (not the character) or because *you*, the actor, don't know what else to do. This is so commonplace that I sometimes threaten to staple my students' feet to the floor! (I don't actually do it…) Inexperienced actors feel that they must be moving to be interesting.

**The Bottom Line:**

> It's okay to be still. There is power in stillness. It's also good to move, but if you are going to move, make sure your movement has purpose. Which brings me to my next point…

## Scene vii

### TOWARDS, AWAY, OR STOP IN PLACE?

No matter how long you have been an actor, training should never stop. We have much to learn, and there are always new and exciting ways of working to be discovered. This has undoubtedly been the case for me as I work with Tom Stroud. Because he has extensive training in both theatre and dance, he approaches actors in motion in a unique way.

In a workshop, Tom made a comment that was so simple. He pointed out that in a scene, actors move in one of three ways: ***toward, away, or stop in place.*** He claimed that the *stop-in-place* is usually short-lived because a masterful actor is always in the process of transitioning, looking for the next place to go.

I decided to experiment with his theory in the last show I directed. At first, I had the ensemble work physically, using the three ways of moving (or not moving) without using text. Then, we added text. After that, we applied Tom's theory to one of the scenes we were blocking. I reminded them they could only move towards, away, or stop in place. It took them a while to catch on, but once they did, it was transformative!

After that rehearsal, I started to observe people: at Walmart, in my classes, at home with my kids, and even at a house party. Tom's theory proved to be true. For instance, when someone was annoying someone else or was frustrated or angry with them, the person on the receiving end tended to move away and create space between them. When they wanted to comfort or confront another person, they moved toward that person. When either of them wanted to figure out what their next move would be, there was a transition in place. They would stop momentarily, and then the whole dance would begin again.

It sounds like common sense—and it is. But applying it to a scene changed how my actors thought about blocking. It motivated their movement and made their blocking feel more organic. It was also exciting to watch.

## Scene viii

### CAT AND MOUSE

When I'm directing a scene, the question I most often ask is, "Who is the cat and who is the mouse?" Another way to put it is, who is driving the scene? The power dynamic can change on a dime. Do you start as a cat and, by the end of the scene, become the mouse?

People with power and status don't need to move a whole lot; people with low status and little power tend to move more. Like the Royals, for example. When waving to the crowd, only one arm and hand are in motion. Every movement is deliberate and necessary; they are never doing more than they have to do.

For the most part, the cat does most of the "toward," and the mouse does much of the "away." The stop-in-place happens when the hunter and the prey assess their next move, or the cat captures their prey. But, even when the cat manages to capture his prey, he doesn't immediately go in for the kill. He plays around with the mouse for a bit and then sits back and contemplates his next move before he pounces. The cat enjoys the hunt as much as he enjoys the kill.

## Scene ix

### NON-VERBAL COMMUNICATION

In the 1970s, professor of psychology Albert Mehrabian studied the importance of non-verbal communication and introduced a communication model he referred to as 7-38-55. His model demonstrated that only 7% of what we communicate conveys the literal content of the message.

Our voice, our tone, our intonation and our volume make up 38% and as much as 55% of our communication consists of our body language. This is incredibly important information for actors!

Although this theory is now considered oversimplified, much of it still holds true. Researchers today would argue that it is accurate only if we focus on emotional communication, although in my view, all communication is emotional.

The important takeaway here is that most people don't realize that much of our communication is non-verbal. If you don't believe me, go to a bar twenty minutes before closing and see for yourself. I can say with great certainty that you will *see* a whole lot of communication going on without a single word being spoken. Most of our communication happens with our bodies, not our words. One person stares across the room at another. He smiles in response, looks away shyly, or maybe walks away uninterested. We speak volumes by twirling a strand of hair around our fingertips, crossing our arms across our chest, or giving someone the stink-eye. What about a teen yelling and screaming "I'm not mad" as she stomps around the house?

***You are what you do, not what you say.*** If someone gets on the bus, walks aggressively to their seat and slams their backpack down beside them, they don't have to say a thing; we know they're not up for some friendly chit-chat. No one has to tell us someone is sad if we notice that their head is hung low, their shoulders are slumped forward, and they're dragging their feet. We see it. That is why actors must be astute observers of human behaviour. People-watching is part of our job.

If you are playing a confident CEO, for example, your body language and your actions need to convey your status to the audience. Having said that, just because you are in a high-power position does not mean you have loads of confidence, and just because you are on the low end of the pay scale does not mean you lack confidence. There are plenty of super-confident janitors, waiters and fast-food employees. And many police officers and lawyers that are not.

**The Bottom Line:**

> The actor's body conveys so much to the audience. Status, approximate age, state of mind, vulnerability, and so much more. The way we move in the world says a great deal about who we are.

## Scene x

### PAUSES AND SILENCES

*"Silence is very important. The silences between the notes are as important as the notes themselves."*
*—Wolfgang Amadeus Mozart*

Everyone on stage has a purpose. When doing scene work, my students often ask, "Can we cut this character out? They only have two lines." Even if the character you are playing has *no* lines, they are on stage for a reason.

In Sarah Delappe's Broadway hit *The Wolves,* for example, the goalie on a young women's elite soccer team barely speaks until the end of the play. During team warmups, she constantly runs off to the bathroom to vomit. As the story unfolds, we realize she is an overachiever who is so paralyzed with performance anxiety that she literally cannot speak. Her silence speaks volumes.

Near the end of the play, there is a scene where she is alone on stage and has a complete emotional breakdown, again, without uttering a single word. She yells, she melts down, she cries, yet she says nothing. When the goalie finally speaks, it is because her meltdown has allowed her to release all of that pent-up anxiety and pressure. Once she lets the air out of the balloon, she has quite a bit to say, and because we have waited so long to hear her speak, we hang on to her every word.

Her silence through most of the play is her story. Her presence without dialogue in every scene is critical to understanding her journey.

**The Bottom Line:**

Whether a character has two lines or no lines at all, they are essential to the scene, or the playwright wouldn't have bothered to include them. Ask yourself what purpose they serve.

# ACT V: "THE PLAY'S THE THING"

## Scene i

### DRAMATIC STRUCTURE

### Freytag's Pyramid of Storytelling

To analyze a scene and chart your character's journey in a play, it is helpful to first understand how a play is structured. Most of us were introduced to basic dramatic structure at some point in a high school, but it won't hurt to do a little refresher before jumping in.

In 1863, a German playwright and novelist named Gustav Freytag transformed Aristotle's dramatic structure into a more detailed, much improved nineteenth-century version, which came to be known as ***Freytag's Pyramid.***

Although Freytag's pyramid of dramatic structure was initially designed for classical tragedies, it has been embraced by novelists, screenplay writers, and playwrights ever since. If we look closely at Freytag's framework, we can see that it includes many of the ingredients in the well-made play. The difference is that Freytag names the points specifically and plots them on a pyramid-shaped graph—a dramatic map, so to speak.

He was obviously on to something because his structure has stood the test of time, particularly in the West. Besides expanding the points from 5 to 7, the structure has remained pretty much the same.

1. Introduction /Exposition
2. Inciting Incident (not originally included in Freytag's Pyramid)
3. Major Dramatic Question (also not originally included in Freytag's structure)
4. Rising Action
5. Climax
6. Falling Action
7. Resolution

Since *Little Red Riding Hood* is a fairy tale familiar to most of us and has a simple story structure, we will use it as our point of reference as we move through the points on Freytag's Pyramid.

## Introduction/ Exposition

As we discussed earlier, exposition is the necessary information the audience needs to follow the story. It usually happens in the introduction of a play but may also be revealed throughout the entire play. This is what Stan referred to as the *given circumstances.* The given circumstances reveal "where" and "when" the story takes place. Are we in a rural farming community in Manitoba during the Great Depression? Are we in a German prison camp during the Second World War? Are we in a confessional in a Catholic church in the middle of the night?

The setting, place and time are critical information for the actor and the audience. The more specific the who, what and where and when, the more it feeds the actor's imagination and invites the audience into the world of the play.

The exposition also introduces us to the major players in our story and their relationships with one another. This may be accompanied by some backstory, particularly for the protagonist. It sets the tone and mood. Is the play a tragedy, a comedy, or a combination of the two (dramedy)? More specifically, is it a farce, a dark comedy, or a rom-com?

### Little Red

Let's examine the exposition in *Little Red Riding Hood:*

**Who?** A young girl (Little Red) and her mother. (No mention of a baby daddy.)

**Where?** They live in a small village on the edge of a forest, presumably somewhere in Europe.

**What?** Mom sends Little Red off to visit her sick Granny and to deliver a basket of goodies.

**Genre?** Fairy tale / European folktale.

### Inciting or Initial Incident

The inciting incident is the catalyst for action, propelling the story forward in dramatic fashion. It is an event (usually involving the protagonist) that hooks the audience in: A woman wakes up and discovers a suicide note on the bedside table, penned by her husband. In *The Wizard of Oz*, Dorothy is swept away by a cyclone. In the case of Little Red, the inciting incident occurs when her mother sends her off into the woods alone (uh-oh) to deliver a basket of goodies to her sick G-ma.

### Time Constraint

Although *time constraints* do not appear on the pyramid, counting down on a clock adds a sense of urgency and dramatic impact to any story. For example, the Fairy Godmother warns Cinderella that she must leave the ball before midnight. If she does not, when the clock strikes twelve, her beautiful ball gown will turn to rags, her carriage into a pumpkin, and her horses into mice.

## The Dramatic Question

Any riveting play should raise many questions, but one needs to stand out above the rest. This question is called the ***major dramatic question***. The *inciting incident* should lead us directly to that question. The initial incident and the dramatic question that follows should happen sooner rather than later, or the writer risks losing their audience. Think of the dramatic question (or D.Q., as I like to call it…because I like ice cream) as the heart of the story. Without it, the audience will not be invested in the outcome.

In the television show *The First 48*, a murder (inciting incident) leads to the dramatic question.

Will the detectives be able to solve the crime within that forty-eight-hour window, or will the murder remain unsolved? When Dorothy is swept up in the cyclone, we want to know if she and poor Toto will make it out alive. When Little Red heads off into the forest alone, we ask ourselves if she will make it to G-ma's house safely. The audience member's desire to answer the dramatic question keeps them invested in the story.

Having said that, the answer to the dramatic question is often apparent. In a rom-com, for instance, we know the two lovers will hook up in the end. The writer then, must make the *how* as interesting as possible. The audience needs to believe (okay, sort of believe) that there is a possibility (however remote) that the relationship may fail.

Conversely, streaming services are so popular because they have been turning formula writing on its head. These shows are like crack because the writers ask dramatic questions that drive us not only to watch an episode but to binge-watch an entire series… sometimes in one weekend… (not that I would know anything about that). Just when we think we have it all figured out, these master carrot-danglers slam on the brakes and take us in a completely different direction. Viewers have become so invested in answering the dramatic question that they have created the term "spoiler alert" so we can warn our friends not to spill the tea.

## Rising Action

Rising action refers to the acceleration of action following the initial incident. In other words, all the stuff that happens once the dramatic question has been posed builds to the climax. The greater the rise, the greater the fall. The protagonist has a major complication that needs to be solved. The journey to solving that problem (rising action) must include built-in tension and momentum on the climb to the top (climax).

The rising action in our fairy tale begins when Little Red runs into the Big Bad Wolf in the woods. Although her mom tells her to stick to the path, the wolf convinces her she should take the long way so she can stop to pick some flowers for her G-ma along the way. This, of course, allows the wolf to take the shorter path so he can get to G-ma's house first. Things really start to cook when the wolf highjacks Granny's P.J.s, jumps into her bed and pretends to be her. The rising action, then, involves all the *obstacles* placed before Little Red as she makes her way to G-ma's house to deliver her basket of goodies. The story must never tread water. Everything that happens must work to move the story forward.

There are, no doubt, some serious holes in this fairy tale, like the wolf deciding not to chow down on Red when he first sets eyes on her. Why does he need to go to Granny's house to do the deed? An obvious story flaw… But I digress…I probably shouldn't be questioning the dramatic structure of a classic European folktale that dates back to the tenth century!

## Climax

The climax is the point of no return, the point at which the subtext becomes context. Things are no longer implied; they are said. The dramatic question is finally answered. This is the moment in the play where the fate of the protagonist is decided, the climax. The final dialogue between Little Red and the Big Bad Wolf in the Brothers Grimm version goes something like this:

LR: Oh, Grandmother, what big ears you have.

BBW: The better to hear you with, my dear.

LR: But, Grandmother, what big eyes you have.

BBW: The better to see you with, my dear.

L.R: But, Grandmother, what large hands you have.

BBW: The better to hug you with, my dear.

LR: Oh, but, Grandmother, what a terrible big mouth you have.

BBW: The better to eat you with.

There is definitely an acceleration in the intensity of the dialogue, but the greatest point of tension occurs when the wolf is about to make a meal of Little Red. In the Brothers Grimm version of the story, he eats poor G-Ma whole before Little Red even shows up. When she does, he eats her, too—end of story. Or is it? This brings us to the next point on our pyramid.

## Falling Action

Falling action occurs as a result of the climax. Once the dramatic question has been answered, any playwright worth the ink cartridge in her printer knows they need to move quickly toward the finish line. As one of my favourite Canadian playwrights, Vern Thiessen, once advised, "Get in late; get out early." In other words, don't start your story at the beginning; start somewhere in the middle. Once the climax has been reached, and the dramatic question answered, get the hell out of Dodge.

The falling action in *Little Red Riding Hood* would be the woodsman hearing the wolf snoring (it's a fairy tale, people!) and then bursting into Grandma's cottage just in time to save the day. When he discovers the BBW in G-ma's bed, he suspects the wolf may have eaten her, so he grabs a pair of scissors and slices open the wolf's stomach. (Not exactly bedtime reading for a little kid!)

Lo and behold, not only is G-ma in there, but also Little Red. Who knew?! The two are a little shaken up, but otherwise perfectly fine.

When looking for the falling action, you need to pinpoint the moment where the protagonist solves the problem, resulting in catharsis, where the tension dissipates. If you pop a balloon with a pin, the pop would be the climax, and the air draining out would be the falling action.

In *Little Red Riding Hood,* this occurs when the wolf is thwarted, and Little Red is reunited with her G-ma.

## Denouement/Resolution

The resolution should be short and sweet. It is the playwright's last opportunity to tie up any loose ends. In our fairy tale, we presume both G-ma and Little Red live happily ever after. This is evidenced by G-ma and G-daughter happily scarfing down cake after the big rescue. Another indication that we are at the end is that the dramatic question has been answered. Although Little Red has successfully overcome a few hurdles (like being devoured by a wolf), she is actually successful in achieving what she set out to do, which was to get the basket of goodies to her sick Granny's house.

## Last Words on Freytag's Dramatic Structure (I Promise)

As a playwright, I often think of Freytag's Pyramid as a pot of water on the stove. When we turn the element on, that is the introduction; as the pot starts to boil, that is the rising action, and when the pot boils over that is the climax. You know we are into the falling action when there is still water bubbling but the water is moving toward stillness. The resolution is when the element has been turned off, and the water returns to its original resting state.

When we break down the pyramid into percentages, old-school playwrights will spend roughly 25% of their time on exposition, 50% on the rising action and climax (the meat of the story), and 25% on the falling action and conclusion. More and more, new writers are embracing the "get in late, get out early" principle. A revised breakdown might be 10–15% on the introduction, 65–75% on the rising action and climax and 10–15% on falling action.

## Conventional Division of a Play

Let me preface everything I have said in this chapter by reminding you that Freytag's Pyramid is a very white, Western, male-centred framework and should be used only as a guide. A playwright may choose to trash division altogether by eliminating scenes and acts, or they may change the sequence of events, resulting in a non-linear story. Sometimes a writer will begin at the end. Others may choose to write a script that moves the story forward predominantly through movement rather than dialogue.

However, most contemporary Western writers hit some or all of the points on the pyramid. Personally, when I hit the wall as a playwright, I go back to Freytag's original recipe to look for an ingredient I may have overlooked.

As we close out this chapter, I hope you see the importance of understanding dramatic structure. Having this knowledge is essential and will help you track your character's journey. It will also illuminate the dramatic arc of the play, even when the playwright has thrown out the rule book!

There are endless ways in which to tell a story, and we need to make room at the table to hear the voices and stories of all people, rather than a select few. That being said, we can learn a great deal from the master playwrights of the past.

## Scene ii

### PUNCTUATION: SIGNS ON THE ROAD

No one said it better than Willy the Shake: "The play's the thing." And because *the play's the thing,* everyone involved with a production should have the playwright's intent at the forefront of their minds. The director, for example, shouldn't be directing a play as a parody if it was meant to be a tragedy. Not only does the director need to know the play intimately, but the entire team does as well. What are the themes in the play? What is the playwright trying to say? Where do the scenes take place? How will the actors transition from one place to another? Ultimately, the job of the creative team is to serve the playwright.

Because playwrights own their work, no changes may be made to the script without the playwright's consent. Conversely, in film, the screenplay writer sells the rights to their work to a movie studio. Once they do that, anything goes. Few film scripts remain untouched after they are given the green light (unless you're Steven Spielberg or Quentin Tarantino). Sometimes, the writer's work is unrecognizable by the time it hits the movie theatre. This is not the case with theatre. In the theatre, we honour thy playwright.

Actors are no exception. They, too, are there to serve the playwright. As a playwright, I often see actors and directors ignoring what I have written, which, if I'm being honest, irritates me a little…okay, maybe a lot. It may seem petty, but when they change my words or ignore my punctuation, it changes the meaning behind what I have written. So, before taking a deep dive into scene analysis, let's chat about why punctuation is so important.

Honouring the punctuation is part of honouring the playwright's intent. I would even go one step further and say that punctuation is just as important as the words themselves. In theatre, ***the script is our road map.*** Like a roadmap, the script tells us everything we need to know to get us where we need to go. Think about it this way: if you are heading out on a road trip to a place you have never been before, would you guess how to get there, or would you use navigation to reach your destination? For most of us (especially me, because I get lost in the grocery store parking lot), using navigation is a no-brainer.

And if the script is our road map, then punctuation is all the signs we encounter along the way: stop signs, speed limits, exit ramps, school zones, etc. If you run a stop sign or speed with no regard for the speed limit, someone will get hurt or, at the very least, earn themselves a speeding ticket. Turning a blind eye to punctuation is like ignoring the rules of the road. Those signs are there to guide you.

The absence of road signs tells us something, too. If a character has a monologue with no periods, we need to flag that. We need to ask ourselves why. Maybe that character is rambling, maybe they never shut up, or maybe their life is in danger. A lack of punctuation may also be a clue to the character's emotional state. Punctuation (or lack thereof) serves multiple purposes. It indicates emphasis, tone, rhythm, pace, and characterization.

If a playwright italicizes something, bolds a word, or uses caps, you need to honour that. In my play *Jail Baby* (co-written with Hope McIntyre, Scirocco Drama, 2013), the Ring Master (the voice of the conservative right) speaks only in capital letters.

> MENTAL ILLNESS, ADDICTION
> NOT ON MY DIME
> IGNORE COLONIZATION
> GET TOUGHER ON CRIME!

The caps suggest the Ring Master speaks with intensity, as if through a megaphone. That is to say, THE RINGMASTER WILL NOT BE IGNORED!!! Does it feel like I'm yelling at you? Because I kind of am.

Punctuation not only reveals the cadence with which a character speaks, but it also speaks to the pacing and given circumstances of the scene. If your character has a gun to his head, for example, the rhythm of the dialogue will differ significantly from that of someone on their deathbed, uttering their final words. All of this is flagged in the punctuation, which is why *it is just as important to memorize your punctuation as it is to memorize your lines.*

Here's an example of two lines that are the same except for the punctuation:

VIOLET: Oh my God she's dead I can't believe she's really dead!!

VIOLET: Oh. My. God. She's dead. I can't believe…she's really dead.

The first version sounds like the character might be a bit hysterical, and the second sounds as if the speaker is in shock. Changing the punctuation changes the meaning and rhythm of the text.

When you memorize your punctuation as well as your lines, it is important that you honour what the playwright has written. Don't add or subtract punctuation; don't add pauses or punch words that aren't punched in the script. Don't ignore overlapping dialogue, silences or pauses.

**The Bottom Line:**

The playwright has given their character a specific rhythm or way of speaking. When you ignore punctuation, you ignore the music within the dialogue.

**TRY THIS:**

When you are first learning your lines, say all of your punctuation out loud along with the text. That way, it will be embedded in your brain.

**AND THIS:**

I highly recommend that you memorize without expression (whispering helps). Only concern yourself with ***what you are going to do with your line, not how you are going to say it.***

If you memorize how you will say a line, you lock yourself into a line read, and that means you are no longer directable.

**AND THIS:**

A great way to practise punctuation awareness is to read a children's book aloud. My personal favourites are those written by Robert Munsch and Dr. Seuss. I use their stories in my university classes, first because they have a truckload of punctuation and second because they are a blast to read.

**AND THIS:**

Read one of Dr. Seuss's masterpieces to a preschooler. A small child is the ultimate test of your dramatic skill. Their attention span is practically non-existent. If you follow the punctuation meticulously and with wild abandon, I guarantee that kid will hang on to your every word.

## A Punctuation Revolution

I am not the only playwright on the planet who is picky about punctuation. In the past forty years, renegade playwrights such as Caryl Churchill began using punctuation as a theatrical device. Instead of a character politely waiting for another character to finish speaking (as was common in the well-made play), her characters interject, interrupt and talk over one another. There are times when five characters are speaking all at once!

Churchill certainly wasn't the first playwright to use overlapping dialogue, but she wields it masterfully, using it as a theatrical device to create specific dramatic effects. Her methods of punctuation are now widely used by playwrights around the globe. Inadvertently, Churchill started a punctuation revolution that is still raging today.

The most obvious purpose of overlapping text is to create realistic dialogue. In real life, we often don't wait our turn to speak. When characters talk over one another, their stories intertwine, and it tells us a great deal about them.

Churchill is known for brilliantly arranging her dialogue as a composer might arrange music, with certain bits of dialogue standing out from the rest. To the ear, it is similar to hearing a symphony orchestra play. At times, it is chaotic, but it is an arrangement of music that interweaves the dialogue in a profound way.

The following are examples of innovative uses of punctuation for dramatic effect:

**Forward Slash** (/)or Double Forward Slash (// ) (Sometimes referred to as a "railroad tracks.")
A forward slash or a double forward slash in the middle of a line of dialogue indicates the character with the following line should

begin speaking, even though the character with the slash in the line hasn't finished speaking.

### Absence of Punctuation at the End of a Line:

If there is no punctuation at the end of a line, that character should continue to their next line without pause. As if the other character has no line at all.

### The Greater-Than Symbol

The greater than symbol (>) works in much the same way. If it appears at the end of a line the actor continues to their next line without pausing.

### Square Brackets

Square brackets indicate what the character is thinking or what a character leaves unsaid. Lines inside these brackets are never spoken aloud.

### Dialogue Running in Parallel Columns

If the playwright has two or more parallel columns with multiple characters, that indicates that all of the characters are speaking at the same time.

### Asterisks*

The asterisk at the end of a line means the character with an asterisk at the beginning of a line will begin speaking (even if that asterisk does not appear until the middle of the next page), again ignoring any dialogue in between.

Let's look at a few excerpts from *BANG BANG*, a hugely successful play by Canadian playwright Kat Sandler. She, too, uses punctuation as a theatrical device. Note that Kat's title *BANG BANG* is in all caps. What does that tell you?

### Small Caps

Sandler not only uses slashes and asterisks, but she also invites the actor to consider punctuation in a whole new way. For example, when we see a line in all caps, most actors see this as an invitation to pump up the volume. Sandler instructs us to think of caps in terms of intensity rather than volume. I would say the same thing applies to exclamation marks. So often, exclamation points are interpreted as an invitation to yell rather than increase intensity.

LILA: With all due respect, fuck your play.

TIM: Jesus, what do you *want?*

LILA: **I WANT YOU NOT TO MAKE THE MOVIE!**

TIM: **WELL I WANT TO MAKE THE MOVIE!** I want to tell a story that leaves you fucking breathless, that pummels your heart until it's a bloody pulp! You are attacking my freedom of speech.

### In-Bracket Line

Another innovative way she uses punctuation is with parentheses. (   ) The person with the parentheses quickly "tucks" in their dialogue with no overlap. For example:

LILA: Let's all read it. Right now. Out loud. (TIM: Umm…) Tim wants me to read it— (TIM: I didn't mean read it out loud!) —Jackie has a bunch of questions about the character's motivation. (JACKIE: I do!) *(to KAREN) You've* already seen it, you know what happens, so really me and Tony are the only ones in the dark…

Lila wouldn't pause for Tim or Jackie's line, but Tim and Jackie would get as close to overlapping as possible without actually overlapping. It's as if Tim and Jackie's lines were a part of Lila's speech.

### Sandler Reconsiders Beats & Ellipses

There is certainly nothing new about using beats or ellipses in a play. What is different is how Sandler asks us to think about them:

### Beat

"It can be a pause or a breath, an extended silence. Whatever the choice, the beat should affect the rhythm of the dialogue."

### Ellipsis ...

"Although it means searching for a thought, it is not a license for a long pause or beat."

(I am so with her on this one!)

The examples of new and exciting ways to use punctuation above are just a small sample of the kinds of punctuation you may encounter in a contemporary play. That is why you should make a habit of reading the playwright's notes before reading the play. Imagine the results of ignoring the punctuation. You would not only be disregarding the playwright's intent, but you would also be putting the rhythm and pacing of the entire play in jeopardy. While punctuation may have a consistent meaning in literature, the use of punctuation in a script may mean different things to different playwrights.

## Scene iii

### CAIRN'S SUPER-SECRET RECIPE FOR SCORING YOUR SCENE

The final assignment for my Intro to Theatre students is to write an in-depth personal essay describing their journey through their first year of performance. Over the years, I have read hundreds of these essays, and 90% begin something like this: "I had no idea acting was so complicated…." The truth is, I felt much the same way in my first year, especially regarding scene analysis.

If analyzing a scene seems like a daunting task, let me reassure you that by the time I finished my honours degree, I had fallen deeply in love with the process. I kid you not; nothing pumps me up more than sitting down with a script and tearing it apart. There are so many questions, and the answers are hidden in the script like buried treasure, which is why you need to approach your text as if you are Sherlock Holmes solving a murder mystery.

Let's pretend for a moment that you are a detective. What do you think your most valuable tool might be? I would have to go with curiosity, relentless curiosity. Make zero assumptions. When we assume, we get tunnel vision and miss important clues. Your beginner's mind is essential to quality sleuthing. If the playwright is skilled, most answers will not be handed to you on a silver platter. If the play is brilliant, each time you read it, you will discover new clues, and it is in these glorious moments of discovery that you will feel like Sherlock Holmes discovering a secret door.

Now that you know how much fun an actor's homework can be, grab your magnifying glass and let's start sleuthing. Remember that reading a play is quite different from reading a novel because ***a play is meant to be seen and heard, not read.*** The words in a novel provide tons of detail, but a play requires the reader to fill in the blanks—to use your imagination. A playwright provides a skeleton, and the actor provides the flesh. Because most of us aren't schooled in reading plays, it's a skill we must develop, but I promise you, the more you do it, the easier and more rewarding it becomes.

## Ingredients for Sleuthing

- Your script (obviously), printed out so you have a hard copy you can write on.
- A pencil (Always a pencil.)
- A big fat eraser (Actors and directors tend to change their minds—a lot.)
- A ruler (Especially if you're a neat freak and need straight lines.)
- Several fine-tipped markers (In a variety of colours.)

## 13 Steps to Scoring a Scene

- ☐ Read the Play!
- ☐ Read the Scene
- ☐ Mark Your Punctuation
- ☐ Given Circumstances
- ☐ List Major Events
- ☐ Literal Action
- ☐ Objective or Underlying Desire
- ☐ Super-objective
- ☐ Mark Unit Changes
- ☐ Name Each Unit
- ☐ List All of Your Unit Words in Sequence

- ☐ Two-Word Journey
- ☐ Title the Scene

### Step 1: Read the Play!

To score a scene successfully, you must familiarize yourself with the play first. The first time you read it through, I recommend you do it in one sitting. Don't burden yourself with analysis; follow the story. The second time around, you can dig a little deeper. Read the play at least three times. Then, and only then, are you ready to narrow your focus to individual scenes.

### Step 2: Read the Scene

Then, read it again and again, now paying more attention to detail. Treat each scene like a slice of pie…a slice of saskatoon berry pie à la mode. (Now I'm hungry.) If you attempt to eat (analyze) the whole play in one sitting (although tempting), it is sure to give you a tummy ache, so let's savour one slice (scene) at a time.

As you read through the scene, note any words or references in the text you don't understand and look them up. That is why Google was invented!

### Step 3: Mark Your Punctuation

Before marking your punctuation, it is imperative that you read Act V, Scene ii: Honour Thy Playwright, The Importance of Punctuation first.

Once you have a hard copy of the scene, get out that red pen (or any other colour that brings you joy) and start bolding your punctuation.

### How to Mark Your Punctuation

Bold all of your punctuation that ends a complete thought. A complete thought is when you see a period, question mark, exclamation mark or colon. I refer to a complete thought as a "full stop." You can bold all of your punctuation in red, or you can bold different kinds of punctuation in various colours. For example, you might bold all of the "full stops" in red and all the half stops (commas and semi-colons) in yellow. Whatever colour you choose, make sure the punctuation jumps off the page.

If a word is bolded, *italicized*, or in CAPS, draw a box around the word you wish to highlight so it stands out on the page.

If there are slashes (/) or greater-than symbols (>), circle them.

You can also circle words or phrases that are repeated. If a playwright repeats something, it is not because they ran out of words; it is because they are trying to tell you something. It is your job to figure out what that *something* is.

Don't add pauses and commas where there aren't any, and don't punch words that aren't punched in the script. If you do, you are messin' with the music! (It's kind of like changing the notes in a musical score.)

**The Bottom Line:**

> Remember, memorizing your punctuation is just as important as memorizing your lines!

## Step 4: Given Circumstances or "W4"

Context is everything, which is why you must first address the given circumstances of your scene.

- Who am I?
- Where am I?
- What the heck is going on? (The events)

Where is the conflict? Or better yet, *what is* the conflict? If you can't find any, you need to dig deeper. Without conflict (including internal conflict), there is no scene. Imagine *No Country for Old Men* without Anton Chigurh? *Batman* without the Joker? *Return of the Jedi* without Darth Vader?

Where is the climax? At what point is the pot of water on the stove boiling over? When you find it, make note of it. Sometimes, it is obvious; other times, you will be scratching your head. The search is half the fun.

### Where Am I Coming From and Where Am I Going To?

When examining given circumstances, one must also include entrances and exits. I once had a director tell me the most impactful moments on stage are a character's entrances and exits. *How* you enter or exit a scene tells us so much about you. So, when analyzing a scene, you need to ask yourself two questions: Where am I coming from, and where am I going to?

Answering these questions will give you the information you need to make informed character choices. It will, for example, tell you how your character might enter or exit the scene. Are you late for something important? Does your character enter having narrowly escaped a barrage of bullets? What if you are a young mother entering the nursery for the first time after losing your newborn child? How would returning to your childhood home after twenty years affect your entrance? Were your memories happy or traumatic? Events such as these determine the way we enter a room. If an actor is pounding on the door before entering that would indicate a sense of urgency. First impressions are lasting impressions.

Where is your character going after the scene ends? Are they off to slay a dragon? Are you going to confess your love to someone? This would certainly influence *how* you exit the scene. You must also track what happens between one scene and the next, even if your character is not in the scene. Has time passed? Did someone die? All of these things profoundly affect how you enter the next scene.

### Step 5: List Major Events

What is the catalyst for action? What happens? In other words, what is the dramatic action? Finding the major events is much like storyboarding. Let's use *Little Red Riding Hood* as an example again:

## Major Events in *Little Red Riding Hood*

1. Mom asks Little Red to deliver a basket of goodies to her sick G-Ma.
2. Little Red agrees and heads off on her journey through the woods, basket in hand.
3. Little Red encounters the Big Bad Wolf, who suggests she take another path to G-Ma's house.
4. Upon arrival, she discovers it is not G-Ma lying in bed but the Big Bad Wolf (who hasn't eaten lunch).
5. The BBW attempts to eat her.
6. A woodsman arrives just in time to save Little Red from certain death.
7. G-Ma and Little Red celebrate their near-death experiences by chowing down on the goodies in Little Red's basket.

Once you decide on the major events in your scene, write them down. Please note that not all scenes are written linearly. A shorter scene may have one or two events, and a longer scene may have as many as eight or nine. There is no set number.

Another way to break down a scene is to look for a beginning, a middle, and an end. If *A* is the beginning, *B* is the middle, and *C* is the end, how does the playwright get from *A* to *B* to *C*? If you really want to shake things up, work from the end of the scene to the beginning. How does the playwright get from *C* to *B* to *A*? Working backward to the beginning is particularly effective when analyzing the play as a whole. How does the playwright get from the events of the final scene to the very first scene in the play?

## Step 6: Literal Action

*What am I (literally) doing? (A Practical Handbook for the Actor,* page 19) The answer to this question should include every line in the scene. Having said that, there are always exceptions to the rule, depending on the style of the play.

When I ask students to tell me what their literal action is, they often overcomplicate it. Be as specific ("generality is the enemy of all art") as possible. Are you *entertaining* guests? Are you *visiting* your dying mother in the hospital? *Robbing* a bank? Note that the latter three examples include verbs. Always use active language when identifying literal action.

**The Bottom Line:**

> Keep it simple. Little Red Riding Hood is literally ***walking*** to her sick grandmother's house to deliver some food—that's it, and that's all.

## Step 7: Objective or Underlying Desire

The question "What do I want?" (Objective) is the most important in scene analysis because ***everything you do, every single line of dialogue coming out of your mouth, is in pursuance of that goal.*** Your objective is what you are going on stage to accomplish. When stating your objective, always use first-person pronouns like "I am" or "I want." The *why* behind the literal action is where your objective or underlying desire comes into play.

Motivation is key because it's what drives your character to do what they do. You go to a party (even though you hate parties) because your best friend begs you to, and you owe her one. If your literal action is *robbing a bank,* your motivation might be that your rent is due, and you have mouths to feed. Maybe you need cash to support a drug habit, or maybe you're on a Robin Hood mission to steal from the rich and give to the poor. The *why* matters. The person who is literally *eating* dinner in a restaurant may be there because they are hungry or because they are *crushing* on a waiter who works there.

If the literal action in *Little Red Riding Hood* is delivering food to G-Ma's house, what is her objective or underlying desire? She is not just going for a hike in the woods; she has a specific goal. That goal might be *nursing her sick G-Ma back to health.* The objective is always connected to the motivation behind it.

Just like the detective trying to solve a murder mystery, you must always look for your character's motivation because the motivation is the fire behind the action and that fire is what will make you unforgettable on stage.

Finally, I cannot stress enough the importance of choosing an objective that excites you. Your goal needs to compel you to action. for example, Romeo, angered by Mercutio's death, murders Tybalt (Willy the Shake, *R & J*, Act 3, Sc.i.) Now murdering someone may not sound like "fun," but if you are Romeo going on stage to avenge your best friend's death, that is damn exciting to play.

## Step 8: Super-objective

Considering the entire play before looking at scenes specifically will inform your choices for your scene objectives. When you put a puzzle together, don't you look at the picture on the box before you start? As your puzzling progresses, you continue to look at that picture as a point of reference. In the end, looking at the big picture will save you a lot of time because (as I pointed out in Stuff about Stan) every scene objective should lead your character in the general direction of their *super-objective*.

In the opening of the movie *Titanic*, it is obvious our protagonist, Rose, isn't over the moon about her engagement to her fiancé, Cal. She feels so hopeless about the prospect of marrying him that she attempts to jump ship, only to be saved by her soon-to-be lover, Jack. Because Jack comes to her rescue, some might assume Rose's super-objective is all about Jack. If you examine the big picture closely, however, it is evident that her super-objective plays out from the very start, long before Jack is even introduced. No doubt, Jack is a big part of Rose's journey, but Jack or no Jack, Rose wants out of her engagement to Cal.

Her super-objective, then, is something along the lines of *personal freedom and independence*. Rose's desperation makes a whole lot of sense when we consider that the story is set in 1912 when options for single women were extremely limited. Divorcing Cal after marrying him is not a viable option. Divorce laws at the time favoured wealthy men, and since most religions frowned upon it, divorced women were often shunned from their social class and stripped of their respectability. Women who did work to support themselves were either single (old maids) or widows. The stakes for Rose couldn't be higher.

As a side note, analysis rookies often attempt to play a super-objective within a scene. ***Make sure the scene objective you have chosen is achievable within that scene.*** Rose wants more than anything to be free of her fiancé's abuse and control, but it is highly unlikely she is going to accomplish that in one scene unless she throws him overboard. Trying to play a super-objective in one scene is like trying to eat a footlong submarine sandwich in one bite! If Rose throws him overboard, we have a much different tale to tell!

Also worth repeating: All plays are *not* written linearly. Some may even begin with the end. Colleen Murphy's play *The December Man* (2007), based on the December 6th, 1989, shooting of fourteen female engineering students at Montreal's École Polytechnique, begins with (spoiler alert) two grieving parents preparing to take their own lives after losing their son, who suffered from survivor's guilt after the massacre, and took his own life. The story begins with the aftermath of the shooting and works its way back to the day of the shooting itself.

P.S. When you encounter a play out of sequence, you will need to track the timeline.

## Step 9: Mark Unit Changes

***Note:** *Steps 9 and 10 should be done together.*

When doing scene work in class, I often encourage students to do this part of the analysis with their scene partner(s). Not only is it easier, but it's also way more fun. Note that this is not possible in a professional theatre environment, because the rehearsal period is brief. The director will expect you to arrive at the rehearsal hall with your homework completed.

After reading the scene multiple times, go back to the beginning and draw a line across the page (yes, in pencil) wherever you encounter a unit change. To refresh, a unit change usually occurs when:

- A character fails to get what they want and moves on to another tactic
- A tactic is unsuccessful, and the character decides to abandon one objective to pursue another
- A character discovers new information
- A character enters or exits the scene (referred to as a *French scene)*

## Step 10: Name Each Unit

Once you have drawn a line separating one unit from the next, you will need to examine each unit individually Each character who has dialogue in that unit (whether it is two characters or ten) should *choose one word they say that sums up that section.* Then, circle the chosen word in your script.

Once you have chosen and circled your word for that unit change, move on to the next. Both you and your scene partner can have input in deciding where the shifts occur, but please mind your beeswax when it comes to choosing individual words—you choose yours, and they'll choose theirs. Choose a juicy word that reflects the subtext and tickles your sense of play.

Move through the entire scene in this way, drawing a line between units and naming each unit. It takes a while to catch on, but once the light bulb goes on, you can pick up the pace. Breaking down your scene into bite-sized chunks will make it less overwhelming.

When you begin the rehearsal process, you can then approach your scene one chunk at a time rather than trying to focus on the whole scene at once.

### Step 11: List All of Your Unit Words in Sequence

When you finish defining and naming all the units in your scene, write down all of your unit words *in sequence*. The string of words before you should encapsulate your character's journey in the scene from beginning to end.

### Step 12: Two-Word Journey

Choose one word (it doesn't have to be a word you say) that describes how your character is feeling at the beginning of the scene, and another word that describes where your character lands at the end of the scene. This is a quick and easy way to see how your character changes from the beginning of the scene to the end. Sometimes, the change will be small; other times, the difference between your first and last words will be quite dramatic. If both words are similar, it usually means you haven't done your job (or the playwright hasn't done theirs). In either case, you need to go back and reread the scene.

### Step 13: Title the Scene

This ingredient in my recipe has been plucked straight from the political mind of German Marxist poet and playwright Bertolt Brecht (1898–1956). Because Brecht strongly believed that theatre should be a teaching tool based on fact rather than escapism, he invented a theatrical technique called *Verfremdungseffekt* (estrangement effect). Alienating his audience, he argued, would allow them to emotionally distance themselves from the plot and characters so that they could focus solely on the political content.

Brecht's technique cast him in the role of scientist; the play became his lab experiment. According to Brecht, the purpose of theatre was not to entertain but to teach. His goal was for the audience to be so inspired by what they saw and heard that they would leave the theatre determined to act upon what they had witnessed.

One of the many ways Brecht alienated his audience was by titling each scene on a placard, followed by a description of what was about to happen. Brecht was the ultimate spoiler! By revealing the plot ahead of the scene, he thought the audience would not be distracted by the outcome, allowing the "observers" to hyper-focus on his political message.

As a playwright, I, too, title my scenes, but not for political reasons. Since playwrights title their work, and a play is made up of a series of mini-plays or scenes, it makes sense. Titling each scene keeps me in check, reminding me to focus specifically on what each scene is about. I strongly recommend you do the same. When an actor titles a scene, it sums up their character's journey in a personal way.

You can be as silly or serious as you like, depending on the tone and genre of the play. If the play has no scenes, you may want to divide it into French scenes and title them. If there are no French scenes, divide them into larger sections instead. (A French scene, as mentioned previously, is created whenever a character enters or exits.)

### Let the Games Begin!

I could blab all day long about how to analyze a scene, but the only way you are going to learn how to do it *is to do it.* The analysis portion of this chapter is in bolded italics so you can differentiate between the script and my commentary.

## Step 1: Read the Play

***Not part of it, all of it. Then, read it again and again and again. Reading the entire play, in this case, won't be necessary only because in the interest of saving trees I have purposefully chosen the opening scene from a play I wrote called*** **SHIKSA.** ***If you were acting in this play, you would of course read the entire play—more than once. The only other instance where reading the play wouldn't be required is if the scene is considered a "short play" and there are no other scenes.***

***If there is a foreword, read it! (*****SHIKSA** ***has been produced but not published, which is why there is no foreword here.) The foreword is usually overflowing with valuable information about the playwright, the style of the play, and the playwright's intent. You should also read any notes from the playwright.***

## SHIKSA

### CHARACTERS

| | |
|---|---|
| ZACK STEIN | Thirty-something, family lawyer and the only son born to Esther and Abe Stein |
| EMMA McTAVISH | Thirty-something, painter |
| ABE STEIN | Father of Zack |
| ESTHER STEIN | Mother of Zack |

### SETTING

The present, Winnipeg, Manitoba, Canada

### SET

The Shabbat table at the home of Abe and Esther Stein. This table should be central to the set.

### NOTES FROM THE PLAYWRIGHT

*SHIKSA* has been written as "heightened reality," thus, the more truthfully the words are played, the more humour and humanity will be revealed.

A backslash ( / ) in the middle of dialogue indicates that the actor with the following line should begin to speak, resulting in overlapping dialogue. If there is a greater than symbol (>) at the end of a line, the actor should drive through, without pause, to the next line. (Another kind of overlap.)

***The Shabbat table's centrality to the set indicates that Judaism will be at the heart of the story. Critical information regarding style and punctuation is also included.***

### Step 2: Read the Scene

***Read the scene carefully. Then, read it again and again and again. A minimum of three times. It will save you time in the long***

***run. P.S. Ignore the circled punctuation for now. We will discuss marking punctuation in Step 3.***

**_SHIKSA_, Scene One:**

*Late summer. Bocelli blares. ZACK STEIN, a thirty-something, fit, rather handsome man wearing jogging pants and a sweat-stained T-shirt, enters the apartment hallway. What ZACK lacks in height, he more than makes up for in charm and confidence. In his hand is a large envelope. He stops in front of Emma's apartment door. He knocks.*

ZACK: Hello...

*Impatient, he knocks again.*

ZACK: Hello...anybody in there?

*ZACK knocks again. The music stops abruptly. EMMA, face covered in a smattering of oil paint, answers the door.*

EMMA: What!

*They stare at one another.*

ZACK: Oh...hello. You're Emma?

EMMA: I am.

ZACK: Emma McTavish?

EMMA: That would be me.

ZACK: Emma McTavish, 745 Wolseley Avenue, apartment 4B?

EMMA: You can cut the small talk. I know who you are.

ZACK: You / do?

EMMA: Yes, I do and...I'm not going to pay the rent...until you...fix the tap in my kitchen.

ZACK: No, no, you don't / understand

EMMA: We get rid of one neglectful landlord and now we have / another?

ZACK: If you / would

EMMA: I have been waiting three months to have that tap fixed. Damn thing leaks all night…drip, drip, drip—

ZACK: No one should have to live like that—

EMMA: My water bill is through the roof—

ZACK: I can imagine—

EMMA: I haven't had a good night's sleep in God knows / how long.

ZACK: I'm sorry to hear / that.

EMMA: You are?

ZACK: Of course.

EMMA And that is why…I am refusing to pay my rent.

ZACK: Seems reasonable.

EMMA: It does?

ZACK: Sure.

EMMA: Does this mean you're not going to evict me?

ZACK: Why would I do that?

EMMA: *(Spontaneously hugs him.)* Thank you. Thank you very much!

ZACK: *(Caught up in the moment, hugging her back.)* I'm not going to evict you because I'm not your landlord.

EMMA: You're not…what? *(Beat.)* Would you mind removing your hands from around my waist?

ZACK: *(Removes his hands.)* Why don't we start over? Pretend this conversation never happened—

EMMA: What conversation?

*EMMA closes the door. ZACK knocks on the door. EMMA answers.*

ZACK: Hello Emma.

EMMA: Hello.

ZACK: How are you?

EMMA: Good, you?

ZACK: Couldn't be better.

EMMA: I didn't catch your name Mr...?

ZACK: My dad is Mr. I'm just Zack...from a few floors up.

EMMA: Oh. How is it you came to know my name, Zack, from a few floors up?

ZACK: It says so right here on your eviction/notice.

EMMA: Give me that—*(She snatches the envelope.)*

ZACK: They keep putting your mail in my box. In any case... they can't just throw you out...you have some paint on your face...

EMMA: Oh...I was...*(She attempts unsuccessfully to wipe it off.)*

ZACK: Here, let me—

EMMA: Don't...do that.

ZACK: Sorry I—

EMMA: Thanks...for the mail.

*EMMA closes the door. ZACK takes a deep breath and knocks on the door.*

EMMA: Miss me?

ZACK: Yes...I mean no. I mean... you forgot something. *(Pulls keys from the door.)* Your keys...

EMMA: Right... *(Closing door.)* Nice to meet you Zack...

ZACK: Stein—Zack. Stein. Now that you know my name, you should probably go out with me.

EMMA: I should, should I? And why is that?

ZACK: I'm irresistibly charming.

EMMA: Can you put that in writing—?

ZACK: If you want me to—

EMMA: What makes you think I'm available—?

ZACK: Are you—

EMMA: Do I look available—?

ZACK: You're evading my question—

EMMA: You're evading mine—

ZACK: No need to be defensive—

EMMA: I'm not—

ZACK: No—?

EMMA: No.

*Beat.*

ZACK: Are you—

EMMA: Am I what—?

ZACK: Available—

EMMA: Available—?

ZACK: Yes—

EMMA: No—

ZACK: No?

EMMA: Well yes. I'm available BUT—

ZACK: But—?

EMMA: NSD—

ZACK: NSD?

EMMA: Not safe to date. Recently back on the market. Irresistibly charming boyfriend turns out to be less than charming. Should have got the charming part in writing.

ZACK: Look…I thought we could…never mind. It was nice meeting you Emma…enjoy your Bocelli.

*ZACK turns to leave.*

EMMA: You know Bocelli?

ZACK: Not personally, no.

EMMA: Kiss me.

ZACK: What?

*EMMA kisses ZACK on the lips.*

ZACK: That was—

EMMA: I'm sorry, I shouldn't / have

ZACK: Can you do that again?

EMMA: Thought I would fast-forward through most of the first date...

ZACK: Works for me—

*ZACK leans in for another kiss. EMMA stops him.*

EMMA: When I kiss someone I can see right into their soul...

ZACK: You can?

EMMA: Oh yes—one kiss tells me everything I need to know.

ZACK: That's a lot to put on one kiss, don't you think?

EMMA: Did you know a man makes love the way he kisses?

ZACK: No...I didn't...know that. *(Pause.)* Well...how was it?

EMMA: Never hurts to get a second opinion.

*EMMA kisses him again, this time more sensually. Both end the kiss intoxicated.*

ZACK: That was—

EMMA: Goodnight Zack.

*EMMA closes the apartment door.*

ZACK: *(Yelling through the door.)* Goodnight? You can't say goodnight—

EMMA: I just did.

ZACK: Was it the kissing...because I can do better. I'm really a great kisser. / Lots of people have—

EMMA: Just because I kiss you doesn't mean I want to sleep with you.

ZACK: Of course not.

EMMA: So if you were thinking that...

ZACK: I wasn't thinking that…

EMMA: you can stop thinking that right now.

ZACK: I mean, I'd like that…but I wasn't thinking that.

*Bocelli swells. ZACK continues to knock on the door as the lights fade.*

*End Scene*

***Did you carefully read over the scene? More than once? If you didn't, shame, shame, double shame—go back and read it again! If the answer is an enthusiastic "yes," let's move on to Step 3.***

### Step 3: Mark Punctuation

***As you probably noticed when you were reading the scene, I circled and made note of all the punctuation for both Zack and Emma. If the hard copy of your scene is starting to look chaotic, that's awesome! A busy page is the sign of a hardworking actor!***

### Step 4: Given Circumstances / W4

***What are the "4 Ws" of this scene?***

1. WHEN: The present
2. WHO: Emma, a thirty-something painter & Zack, a thirty-something lawyer
3. WHERE: Winnipeg, Manitoba. More specifically, Zack is in his apartment building, in the hallway, knocking on Emma's apartment door.
4. WHAT: What is going on? More on that in step 5.

### Step 5: List Major Events

***1. Zack knocks on Emma's door to deliver mail (an eviction notice) that has mistakenly been delivered to his mailbox.***

***2. Emma, thinking Zack is the new landlord, tells him she is not going to pay the rent until he fixes her leaky faucet. When***

*she finds out he is not going to evict her, she gives him a very enthusiastic hug.*

*3. Zack confesses he is not the landlord. Emma closes the door so they can "start over."*

*4. Zack introduces himself and then suggests Emma should go out with him. Emma rejects his offer, claiming she is "NSD."*

*5. Zack declares defeat and leaves.*

*6. Emma finds out "he knows" Bocelli and impulsively kisses Zack. Because the first kiss was off the charts, she kisses him again.*

*7. Emma puts her impulsivity in check by closing the door in Zack's face.*

*8. Zack tries to get her to open the door. She isn't biting.*

*I have listed eight major events; you may have more or fewer. This scene is written simply, which means the major events are pretty obvious. If you are having trouble deciding what the events in the scene are, read the scene again.*

## Step 6: Literal Action

*What are Zack and Emma literally doing in the scene? Remember, keep it simple.*

EMMA: Considering that literal action should include all or most of the dialogue in the scene, I would say (and I'm right because I wrote it) that Emma is literally trying to get rid of the annoying person at her door, whom she believes to be her new landlord demanding the rent.

ZACK: Zack has come to Emma's apartment to deliver a piece of mail that has been mistakenly delivered to his mailbox. He has no idea who is on the other side of the door. He is literally delivering a piece of mail to his neighbour.

### Step 7: Scene Objective or Underlying Desire

***Determining literal action is like scratching the surface. To find your scene objective, you need to grab a shovel and start digging.***

EMMA: From the opening of this scene, it is clear that Emma wants to get rid of Zack. The important question is why? He seems like a nice enough guy. The answer is multifaceted. Initially, she wants him to leave because she is in the midst of painting; second, she mistakes him for the new landlord, who is there to collect the rent, which she doesn't have. Finally, she is attracted to him and knows dating is not in her best interest right now because she is NSD (Not Safe to Date).

If you were to read the entire play, you would know Emma has recently moved to Winnipeg to get a fresh start and doesn't want "the handsome man from two floors up" to mess that up.

ZACK: Once Emma opens that door and he sees she is an attractive, feisty young woman, and not some nice old lady living in the block, he wants to convince her to go out with him. In a more immediate sense, Zack wants to keep that apartment door open.

Whatever objective you may choose for a scene, keep in mind it must conflict with your scene partner's objective. In this instance, Zack wants to keep the door open, and Emma wants to close it.

The most exciting characters go after what they want in a big way. It's that desire and drive that make a character compelling to watch. Emma has a hard time resisting Zack's charm, which results in some impulsive, unpredictable behaviour: One minute, she is kissing him passionately, and the next minute, she is slamming the door in his face. She is doing her very best to resist temptation. (We don't always get what we want!)

### Step 8: Super-objective

*Since you haven't read* SHIKSA, *I am providing you a brief synopsis of the play so we can discuss super-objectives.*

Play Description: SHIKSA *is a romantic comedy in two acts that explores the inherent challenges of multi-faith relationships and our human need to find a place of belonging.*

EMMA: Super-objective. *As the story progresses, we find out more about Emma's past and her unresolved emotional issues. She grew up without a father; she also carries emotional trauma after being in a tragic car accident with her mother. Her mother does not survive. When it comes to romantic love, she has failed to find her forever person. Once we are acquainted with her backstory, it makes perfect sense that she would be drawn to Zack and, ultimately, to Judaism. Although Zack's family initially rejects her, Emma eventually wins them over.*

*Emma's super-objective is to find a place of belonging. Ironically, she doesn't find that place with Zack, she finds it with Zack's parents. Although Emma gets what she wants, like Rose in* Titanic, *it does not happen in the way she envisions.*

ZACK: Super-objective. *Zack wants freedom, especially when it comes to making his own decisions. Although he doesn't want to completely cut ties with his overprotective parents, he does want them to respect his right to privacy and self-determination. Unlike Emma, he wants to distance himself from his family and his Jewish roots.*

*In other words, Zack is running away from the very thing Emma is running toward. Because Zack feels guilty and is afraid to hurt both his parents and Emma, ultimately, he chooses to keep his relationship with the "shiksa" a secret, and ends up lying to everyone. Judaism, in his mind, is what stands in the way of his freedom.*

*By the end of the play, Zack doesn't attend synagogue every Friday or keep kosher, but he does begin to understand Emma's attraction to Judaism. He learns to respect and honour his family history and opens his mind to what it offers. To take a line from the play, he learns that "Judaism is more about belonging than it is about believing." As his relationship with Emma evolves, he finds a kind of freedom, but like Emma, not in the way he expects.*

## Step 9: Mark Unit Changes & Step 10: Name Each Unit

***Steps 9 and 10 should be done together.***

***Now, it's time to break the scene down into bite-sized pieces. Different actors will have different opinions about where a shift happens. Since I wrote this play, I can provide insight into where the unit changes occur and my reasoning behind them.***

***When a unit ends, draw a line across the page (in pencil). Remember, a unit can happen in silence or even in the middle of a line—enough talking, let's get down to business.***

### *SHIKSA,* SCENE ONE

*Late summer. Bocelli blares. ZACK STEIN, a thirty-something, fit, rather handsome man, wearing jogging pants and a sweat-stained T-shirt, enters the apartment hallway. What ZACK lacks in height, he more than makes up for in charm and confidence. In his hand is a large envelope. He stops in front of Emma's apartment door. He knocks.*

ZACK: **Hello…**

*Impatient, he knocks again.*

ZACK: Hello... anybody in there?

*ZACK knocks again. The music stops abruptly. EMMA, face covered in a smattering of oil paint, answers the door.*

---

***I would draw my first line here. Initially, Zack is alone on stage, envelope in hand, knocking on Emma's door. His literal action is to return the envelope to its rightful recipient. Once that door opens, his objective changes. Adding Emma to the mix changes the dynamic and warrants a shift in tactics.***

***Now that you have drawn a line (in pencil), each character chooses one word they say to encapsulate that section. Sometimes, you have to break the rules and splurge on two words or even a***

***phrase but do your best to stick to the one-word rule. Since Zack is the only character in this section, only he will choose a word.***

## EXAMPLE OF WORD CHOICES

ZACK: **Hello...**

***Including the ellipsis here is important because it suggests he is awaiting a response. Let's move on to the next unit.***

---

EMMA: What!

*They stare at one another.*

ZACK: Oh...hello. You're Emma?

EMMA: I am.

ZACK: Emma McTavish?

EMMA: That would be me.

ZACK: Emma McTavish, 745 Wolseley Avenue, apartment 4B?

---

## EXAMPLE OF WORD CHOICES

EMMA: What!

ZACK: Emma?

***Because two characters are speaking in this section, both Emma and Zack will choose a word. Remember, it is not kosher to influence the other actor's word choice. You worry about your words, and they'll worry about theirs.***

***When Emma answers the door, she is doing so because he won't stop knocking, and she is painting. Also, Emma hasn't paid her rent, so she is avoiding the landlord. When the door opens, Zack is most likely expecting to see a nice old lady on the other side; otherwise, he wouldn't show up in a sweat-stained T-shirt. His original objective of simply delivering the mail changes the second she opens the door.***

---

EMMA: You can cut the small talk. I know who you are.

ZACK: You / do?

EMMA: Yes, I do and…I'm not going to pay the **rent**…until you…fix the tap in my kitchen—

ZACK: **No**, no, you don't / understand

EMMA: We got rid of one neglectful landlord, and now we have / another?

ZACK: If you / would

EMMA: I have been waiting three months to have that tap fixed. Damn thing leaks all night…drip, drip, drip>

ZACK: No one should have to live like that—

EMMA: My water bill is through the roof —

ZACK: I can imagine—

EMMA: I haven't had a good night's sleep in God knows / how long.

ZACK: I'm sorry to hear / that.

EMMA: You are?

ZACK: Of course.

EMMA: And that is why…I am refusing to pay my rent.

ZACK: Seems reasonable.

EMMA: It does?

ZACK: Sure.

---

## EXAMPLE OF WORD CHOICES

EMMA: **Rent**

ZACK: **No**

***Emma assumes Zack is the landlord and try as he may, Zack can't get a word in to tell her otherwise. We also get the impression Emma is making excuses for not paying her rent (leaky tap). Truth be told, she has no money to pay the rent and fears***

***eviction. Although there is a spark between them, this unit is all about the rent for Emma. Zack is simply trying to clear up a misunderstanding, but Emma won't let him get a word in.***

---

EMMA: Does this mean you're not going to **evict** me?

ZACK: Why would I do that?

EMMA: *(Spontaneously hugs him.)* Thank you. Thank you very much!

ZACK: *(Caught up in the moment, hugging her back.)* I'm not going to evict you because I'm not your **landlord.**

EMMA: You're not—what? *(Beat.)*

---

## EXAMPLE OF WORD CHOICES:

EMMA: **evict**

ZACK: **landlord**

***Emma is solely focused on her eviction, and Zack is focused on trying to tell her he is NOT her new landlord; at the same time, he's enjoying that hug and wants to linger in it for a while longer. When Emma finds out he is not her landlord, that new information changes everything.***

---

EMMA: Would you mind **removing** your hands from around my waist?

ZACK: *(Removes his hands.)* Why don't we **start over?** Pretend this conversation never happened—

EMMA: What conversation? *(Closes the door.)*

---

## EXAMPLE OF WORD CHOICES:

EMMA: **removing**

ZACK: **start over?**

***Their tactics drastically change when Emma realizes Zack is not her new landlord. Emma is embarrassed that she has hugged a complete stranger, so asking him to remove his hands from around her waist shifts the focus away from the awkwardness of it all. Since Zack's objective is to ask her out, "starting over" is his best shot at making that happen.***

---

*ZACK knocks on the door, and EMMA answers.*

ZACK: **Hello** Emma.

EMMA: **Hello.**

ZACK: How are you?

EMMA: Good, you?

ZACK: Couldn't be better.

EMMA: I didn't catch your name Mr…?

ZACK: My dad is Mr. I'm just Zack…from a few floors up.

EMMA: Oh. How is it you came to know my name, Zack, from a few floors up?

ZACK: It says so right here on your eviction / notice.

EMMA: Give me that— *(She snatches the envelope.)*

ZACK: They keep putting your mail in my box. In any case… they can't just throw you out… You have some paint on your face…

---

## EXAMPLE OF WORD CHOICES:

EMMA: **Hello**

ZACK: **Hello**

***This beat suggests Emma is intrigued, if not attracted to Zack, otherwise, she wouldn't bother to open the door a second time. She is also embarrassed that Zack knows she has an eviction notice. The focus is now on renewal for both of them. Zack genuinely***

***wants to start over, and "hello" is his entry point, and from there, he pours on the charm.***

***His move to wipe the paint from her face not only warrants a unit change but also allows Zack to take one more step forward in achieving his objective. Put it this way: if a nice old lady had opened that door, I'm pretty sure Zack wouldn't be wiping paint from her face.***

---

EMMA: Oh...I was... *(She attempts unsuccessfully to wipe it off.)*

ZACK: Here, let me—

EMMA: **Don't**...do that.

ZACK: **Sorry** I—

EMMA: Thanks...for the mail.

*EMMA closes the door.*

---

**EXAMPLE OF WORD CHOICES:**

EMMA: **Don't**

ZACK: **Sorry**

***When Zack touches her face to remove the paint, the intimacy of that moment is just too much for Emma. From Zack's perspective, "Don't" may mean he has just blown his chance to get what he wants. Apologizing is a last-ditch effort to keep that door from closing.***

---

*ZACK takes a big breath and knocks on the door. EMMA opens the door.*

EMMA: **Miss** me?

ZACK: Yes...I mean, no. I mean ...you forgot something. *(Pulls keys from the door.)* Your keys...

EMMA: Right... *(Starts closing the door.)* Nice to meet you, Zack...

ZACK: **Stein**—Zack. Stein.

---

## EXAMPLE OF WORD CHOICES

EMMA: **Miss**

ZACK: **Stein**

***"Miss" is an interesting choice for Emma. She knows she needs to shut him down, but Zack's charm keeps her intrigued. Emma has the upper hand here because the decision to open or close the door is entirely within her control. She can afford to be a little cheeky. Zack is becoming more desperate to keep that door open. If she closes it, he wants to be sure she remembers his full name—in case she changes her mind.***

---

ZACK: Now that you know my name, you should probably **go out** with me.

EMMA: I should, should I? And why is that?

ZACK: I'm irresistibly charming.

EMMA: Can you put that in writing—?

ZACK: If you want me to—

EMMA: What makes you think I'm available—?

ZACK: Are you—

EMMA: Do I look available—?

ZACK: You're evading my question—

EMMA: You're **evading** mine—

ZACK: No need to be defensive—

EMMA: I'm not—

ZACK: No—?

EMMA: No.

*Beat.*

## EXAMPLE OF WORD CHOICES

EMMA: **evading**

ZACK: **go out**

***Emma is evading Zack's offer to go out with him. Zack is irresistibly charming, and Emma is determined to resist his charms. She is trying to get her life in order, and the last thing she needs is for some man to come along and ruin everything.***

***Zack could walk away after Emma shuts the door, but he is determined to ask her out. Again, I've broken the one-word rule, but "go out" really sums up not only this section but most of the scene. In desperation, he finally blurts out what he wants.***

---

ZACK: Are you—

EMMA: Am I what—?

ZACK: **Available**–

EMMA: Available—?

ZACK: Yes—

EMMA: No—

ZACK: No?

EMMA: Well, yes. I'm available. BUT...

ZACK: But—?

EMMA: **NSD**–

ZACK: NSD?

EMMA: Not safe to date. Recently back on the market. Irresistibly charming boyfriend turns out to be less than charming. Should have got the charming part in writing.

ZACK: Look...I thought we could—never mind. It was nice meeting you, Emma...enjoy your Bocelli.

*ZACK turns to leave.*

## EXAMPLE OF WORD CHOICES

EMMA: **NSD**

ZACK: **Available**

***Although Emma is attracted to Zack, she knows she is fresh out of a nasty breakup and going out with him is not in her best interest. Zack wants to know if she is available. If she has a boyfriend, he is wasting his breath. When she says she is NSD, Zack accepts defeat and walks away.***

---

EMMA: You know **Bocelli?**

ZACK: Not personally, no.

EMMA: Kiss me.

ZACK: **What?**

*EMMA kisses ZACK on the lips.*

---

## EXAMPLE OF WORD CHOICES

EMMA: **Bocelli?**

ZACK: **What?**

***The mention of "Bocelli" seems to be the catalyst for action (the kiss). The word "What?" expresses his disbelief. Zack just won the lottery! P.S. Note that I have included the punctuation with the word.***

---

ZACK: That was—

EMMA: I'm sorry, I shouldn't / have

ZACK: Can you do that **again?**

EMMA: Thought I would **fast-forward** through most of the first date...

ZACK: Works for me—

---

## EXAMPLE OF WORD CHOICES

EMMA: **Fast-forward**

ZACK: **Again?**

***The kiss changes everything. Zack is completely and utterly gobsmacked by Emma's impulsivity but is obviously an enthusiastic participant. He wants more. Emma is well aware that things are moving too "fast."***

---

*ZACK leans in for another kiss. EMMA stops him.*

EMMA: When I kiss someone, I can see right into their soul....

ZACK: You can?

EMMA: Oh yes...**one kiss t**ells me everything I need to know.

ZACK: That's a lot to put on **one kiss**, don't you think?

EMMA: Did you know a man makes love the way he kisses?

ZACK: No...I didn't... know that. (*Pause.*) Well...how was it?

EMMA: Never hurts to get a second opinion.

*EMMA kisses him again, this time more sensually. Both end the kiss intoxicated.*

---

## EXAMPLE OF WORD CHOICES

EMMA: **one kiss**

ZACK: **one kiss**

***When Zack leans in for another kiss, Emma shuts him down with intimidation. That "one kiss tells her everything" puts a lot of pressure on poor Zack. It also puts Emma back in the driver's seat. Emma's comments about kissing force Zack to focus on his kissing performance. Here again, one word doesn't seem to be enough.***

---

ZACK: **That was—**

EMMA: **Goodnight** Zack.

*EMMA closes the apartment door.*

---

## EXAMPLE OF WORD CHOICES:

EMMA: **Goodnight**

ZACK: **That was—**

***He is mesmerized by her kiss and is more acted upon in this short section. Emma desperately needs to rein in her passion, and the only way she can think of to do that is to put some distance between them, so she closes the door.***

---

ZACK: *(Yelling through the door.)* **Goodnight?** You can't say goodnight—

EMMA: I just did.

ZACK: Was it the kissing…because I can do better. I'm really a great kisser. / Lots of people have—

EMMA: Just because I kiss you doesn't mean I want to **sleep** with you.

ZACK: Of course not.

EMMA: So if you were thinking / that>

ZACK: I wasn't thinking that…

EMMA: you can stop thinking that right now.

ZACK: I mean, I'd like that…but I wasn't thinking that.

*Bocelli swells. ZACK continues to knock on the door as the lights fade.*

---

## EXAMPLE OF WORD CHOICES

EMMA: **Sleep**

ZACK: **Goodnight?**

***Emma has just kissed a stranger. She is an intelligent woman and knows this probably wasn't a great decision, especially when we consider she enjoyed it enough to do it a second time. We sense Emma's way of dealing with intimacy is to shut down. Once again, she backpedals by saying, "Just because I kiss you doesn't mean I want to sleep with you." It is also suggestive.***

***Always ask yourself why your character is making one choice over another. Actions really do speak louder than words. That Emma chooses to continue her conversation with Zack (albeit through a closed door) tells us she is interested in him. Poor Zack can't believe his luck when she kisses him not once but twice! That she wants to say goodnight after a passionate kiss is unthinkable, but at the same time, it draws him in even more.***

---

## Step11: List All of Your Beat Words in Sequence

***After naming all your beats, string all your words together in sequence. If you have chosen wisely, the words should track your character's journey in the scene. Read the words out loud in order.***

| Zack's List of Words | Emma's List of Words |
|---|---|
| Hello | |
| Emma? | What! |
| No… | Rent |
| Landlord | Evict |
| Start over | Removing |
| Hello | Hello |
| Sorry | Don't |
| Stein | Miss Me? |
| Go out | Evading |
| Available | NSD |
| What? | Bocelli |
| Again? | Fast-forward |

| | |
|---|---|
| One kiss | One kiss |
| Goodnight? | Sleep |

***The list of words and phrases encapsulates Emma and Zack's journey in this scene. Choosing a word for each unit allows the actors to track where they start, where they are going, and where they need to land.***

## Step 12: In a Word

***Choose a word (it doesn't have to be a word your character speaks) to describe where your character is emotionally when the scene begins. Choose another word to describe where your character is emotionally when the scene ends. If time is an issue (cold read), this is a quick and efficient way to track your character's journey in a scene.***

## TWO-WORD JOURNEY FOR ZACK & EMMA

EMMA:
(beginning) → (end)
**Annoyed → Infatuated**

ZACK:
(beginning) → (end)
**Interested → Lovesick**

***Emma goes on a journey from "Annoyed" to "Infatuated." Zack embarks on a journey that takes him from "Interested" to "Lovesick." That is a whole lot of dramatic action for one little scene!***

## Step 13: Title the Scene

***In your own words, title the scene. Forget the playwright for a moment and make it personal to your character. Suggestions for a scene title might be:***

***"Boy Meets Girl"***

***"Go Away, Come Back"***

***"Lust at First Sight"***

### The Bottom Line:

Scene analysis takes time and patience. You don't need to do it all at once. Read the play one day, read the scene another, and do the unit breakdown the next. Don't rush. Allow time for contemplation. You want to enter the rehearsal process with a beginner's mind, open to direction and excited to play in the sandbox with your playmates. If you are in a play, break down every scene you are in. Avoid locking anything down. It's common for actors to change their words as they get deeper into the rehearsal process.

If you have to do scene analysis alone, no worries, but whenever possible (especially when you are learning), try and do the shifts/unit changes and word choices with your scene partner.

### TRY THIS:

Choose a scene from one of your favourite plays. Follow all thirteen steps as one character. From the words you have chosen, is your character's journey clear? Are the two words you have chosen for your character quite different? If they are not, repeat the exercise.

# EPILOGUE

## Final Thoughts

*"Parting is such sweet sorrow."*
—R & J, *Willy the Shake*

And now the time has come to bid you all adieu. I'm not so good at goodbyes, so I'll be brief. It has been a pleasure to offer you some guidance on your acting journey. I've been brewing theatre tea for over thirty years, so spilling some of it feels cathartic! Whatever speaks to you from these pages, I hope you put it into practice as you navigate the wacky, unpredictable, wonderful world of theatre. A world that I have not regretted being a part of for a single moment. Theatre has been, and always will be, my passion. I hope it will be yours too.

As our journey comes to an end, I would like to offer you some advice: First, humans are innately creative beings, and we must find avenues for creative expression—acting is a beautiful way to do that. In creation and collaboration, you will make lifelong friends and memories. If you're lucky, you may feel, as I have, that you have finally found your people, your family, a place where you belong.

That is not to say that it will be easy. On your journey, there will be many bumps in the road. Take gentle care. Be kind to yourself. Never stop learning. Embrace every opportunity to continue training, especially in areas that take you outside your comfort zone. Evict all the dream killers from your life. Take a risk every day, and for heaven's sake, give yourself permission to fail—often! And when things get scary (and they will), don't run away. It is when we are on the precipice of self-discovery that we are most likely to self-sabotage.

Learn the art of shameless self-promotion. You're self-employed, which means you are your own cheerleader. It's not like people are going to magically appear like little fairies on your doorstep and offer you work. Early to bed, early to rise, and don't forget to advertise! I used to be shy about putting my artistry out there, but after a few months of being late on my rent, I got over it. Now you can't shut me up! I pride myself on being extra shameless. You never know who you are going to cross paths with. Why miss out on an opportunity?

Above all else, I wish that when you close this book, you will believe wholeheartedly that you are Born Ready—because you are! The biggest hurdle will be convincing yourself of that. If I have failed in making a believer in you, I challenge you to look at yourself directly in your bathroom mirror and say it aloud every morning: "I am Born Ready!" because one of these days, you'll start believing, and the next day, you will believe a little more. Before you know it, a full-fledged believer will be staring back at you.

For those of you who are not in their teens or twenties, it's never too late! Well over half of the students in my theatre school are over the age of thirty-five, including one in his eighties. As I embark on my own final chapter, I care less about what other people think of me. I'm like a small child with no censor. It's very freeing! This sense of newfound freedom is a quality I often observe in my more mature students. As we age, we feel the clock ticking, and we want to relish every moment. There is no longer the luxury of time. We ask ourselves, if not now, then when?

Only a week ago, a seventy-two-year-old retired physician asked me if she was too old to take an acting class. Hell to the no!!! She told me she had always wanted to take an acting class but could never find the time. Now is her time. Young or old, not all of you who read this book are going to run off to New York to pursue a career on Broadway, but I can promise you that all of you who explore acting will be changed in some way by that experience—some profoundly changed.

And now the tears come. (What can I say, I'm a crybaby.) Over the years, I have shed many a tear watching hundreds and hundreds of caterpillars become butterflies. That, my friends, is the magic of theatre. May you relish in your metamorphosis.

# BIBLIOGRAPHY


Adler, Stella, *Creating a Character: A Physical Approach to Acting,* Applause, 1993

Bajer, Sharon, *Behind the Scenes* in J. Gordon Shillingford Publishing newsletter, November 2024

Ball, David, *Backwards & Forwards: A Technical Manuel for Reading Plays,*Southern Illinois University Press, 1983

Bond, Laura, *The Emotional Body*, Pure Expressions, LLC, 2018

Bond, Laura, *TEAM for Actors,* CreateSpace Independent Publishing Platform, October 8, 2012

Bruder, Melissa, *A Practical Handbook for the Actor,* Vintage, 1986

Caldarone, Marina and Lloyd-Williams, *ACTIONS,* QSM/Drama, 2004

Cameron, Julia, *The Artist's Way: A Spiritual Path to Higher Creativity*, Jeremy P. Tarcher, 2002

Delappe, Sarah, *The Wolves,* Harry N. Abrams, 2018

Garton Stanley, Sarah, "Failure Points" in *Canadian Theatre Review*, Vol. 150, 2012

Grimm, Jacob and Wilhelm, *Little Red Riding Hood,* NorthSouth Books, 2018

Hagen, Uta, *Challenge For The Actor,* Scribner, 1991

Haidt, Jonathan, *The Anxious Generation,* Penguin Press, 2024

Intimacy Directors International, *The Pillars: Rehearsal and Performance Practice,* 2016-2020

Meisner, Sanford, *On Acting,* Vintage, 1987

Mulder, P. (2012). *Communication Model by Albert Mehrabian.* Retrieved July 28, 2025 from ToolsHero: https://www.toolshero.com/communication-skills/communication-model-mehrabian/

Murphy, Colleen, *The December Man,* Playwrights Canada Press, 2007

Patterson, Debbie, *Generation NeXt, "Baby Killer Cat Fight"* Scirocco, 2010

Perrault, Charles, *Little Red Riding Hood, and Other Classic Fairy Tales of Charles Perrault,* Penguin Classics, 2008 (originally written in 1697)

Robbins, Mel, *The 5 Second Rule,* Save Republic, 2017

Sandler, Kat, *Bang Bang,* Playwrights Canada Press, 2019

Stanislavski, Konstantin, 1863–1938. *An Actor Prepares.* New York: Theatre Arts, inc., 1936

Strasberg, Lee, *A Dream of Passion: The Development of the Method,* Plume, 1988

Walker, George F, *The Suburban Motel Series,* Talonbooks, 1999

# FLOWERS

I would like to take a moment to send flowers to all of the amazing writers, students and theatre practitioners who held my hand on this journey. Without you, this book would not have come to fruition. You are not just my students, colleagues and friends, you are people that I respect and love. When you were busy with your own lives and pressing deadlines, you showed up for me. In my fortunate experience, that is what theatre people do. We show up for each other.

My girls! You mean everything to me! A ginormous thank you to the members of the WWF (Women Writing Fearlessly): Rebecca Brask, Demetra Hajidiacos, Alison McLean, and Cheyenne Schroeder. I am grateful for your undying support, your generosity in allowing me to monopolize our time for the past couple of years, and the many bottles of Prosecco you supplied in the name of the cause. And let me not forget the love and support from my Yummy Mummies (Kelly Fraser Hunt, Janet McLeod, Heather Scerbo and Char Thompson) and my close girlfriends Marlene-Stage-Goddess-Meaden and Jane Runner. All of you have been showing up for my theatre stuff for as long as I can remember. To my fellow *Goddess Rising* members Arlea Ashcroft and Johanna Stein—where the writing seed was planted.

Thanks to my friend Andrew Davidson, who is not only a *New York Times* best-selling author (*The Gargoyle*) but also an incredibly skilled and insightful editor. Andrew was also a relentless cheerleader throughout the writing process. To Dan Gregovski for digging deep for quotes in the public domain when I ran out of time to do it myself.

Thank you, Rick Skene, for being my most influential teacher while completing my honours degree at the University of Winnipeg. You are the best storyteller ever, and you always created an environment that made me feel safe to fail. I often catch myself repeating your words while teaching a class. You influenced my teaching style more than I knew. It was only when I began writing this book that I realized how much I carry your teachings with me.

Thank you, Raye Anderson, now murder mystery novelist (Signature Editions) for being my boss who never felt like a boss, for fifteen incredible years at Prairie Theatre Exchange. You were patient and kind and taught me how to teach any child or adult who walked through the door. You never hovered. Only guided and inspired.

More recently on my acting journey, I have had the good fortune of training with my most influential mentor—Mr. Tom Stroud. You are my Mr. Miyagi! Making me think, making me reconsider my perspective. Taking me to the edge of the cliff while still holding my hand. Just don't ask me to start painting fences in your backyard! You are the definition of a master teacher. Training with you has been life changing. Watching you work has been life changing. Please continue to blow my mind and challenge me. My greatest wish is to remain open to new ways to work with actors.

Hope McIntyre, the Nellie McClung of theatre, thank you. You were the first to insist that women's voices be heard in theatre in Manitoba. Thank you for being my friend, my colleague, my writing partner and for the many artistic projects we have embarked on together. If Hope is starting a new project, I want to be a part of it because whatever it is, I know it's going to make a difference in the world.

Glenda MacFarlane, my editor: you are so gracious, kind and incredibly skilled at what you do. Patience should be your middle name! I knew we were an awesome pairing when you signed your first email to me with X's and O's. You gave me the room and encouragement to find my voice. Thank you, Karen Haughian, for taking a chance on me. We are so fortunate to have a local publisher dedicated to theatre!

Ginormous hearts to those who have become a part of my theatre family: Anika Binding, Isaac Bonham, Lisa Bryski, Sol Choi, William Carrette, Brandon Case, Corrina Colvinson, Mike Chapin, Nina Eilberg, Sid Fiola, Natasha Fisher, Emily Forrest, Mazi Frank, Dan Gregovski, Vance Halldorson, Kristi Hay, Sophie and Molly Helmer, Brent Hoar, Nora Kroeger, Esther Momtchilov, Pranav Nnair, Ryan Pahl, Leah Peever, Christine Reimer, Sarah Rossen, Shohreh Saeedibagha, Liam Scheirer, Colton Tomchuk, Marc Torchinsky, Elizabeth Walker, Katie Welham, Miss Maia Woods and Seth Yager. Your love of theatre nourishes my soul.

Thank you to my two beautiful and talented children, Cyra and Tamir. In you I see two sensitive kind, creative souls that continue to delight and inspire me profoundly. I'm so proud of both of you. Thank you, Mummy, for the many things you do for me so that I may have more time to create. Thank you to my sister Darlene (whom I affectionally call "Weenie"), who has always been my greatest cheerleader.

The biggest bouquet goes to my incredible husband Jeff, who has taken on the role of IT guy, box office manager (no, you are not getting a raise), and fixer of all things. Thank you for all of the times you listened to me read and reread chapters from this book instead of binge watching a Netflix series or going for a Sea-Doo ride. (No more excuses!) Thanks for loving me extra throughout this writing process.

And last, but definitely not least, my students—Why I am here—Why I continue to be here—Why I can't seem to leave—Why I have written this book. I have written this book for you because you're amazing! You're brave. You're Born Ready! You bring me such joy and purpose. After all these years of teaching and directing, I am still brought to tears every time I witness one of you making a creative discovery, which by the way is often. There is nothing that touches my heart more. So, thank you. Thank you for allowing me to be some small part of that.

## CAIRN A. MOORE

Cairn A. Moore is an actor, director and playwright. She has been teaching and inspiring first-year performance students at the University of Winnipeg for over twenty-five years! She is the former associate artistic director of FemFest and the former associate education director of Prairie Theatre Exchange School. She is also the founder and proud owner of Actors Studio with Cairn Moore. Cairn has co-written two plays with Hope McIntyre: *Jail Baby* (Scirocco Drama) and *Breaking Through* (Sarasvati). She was the editor and contributor for *Generation NeXt,* a collection of juicy scenes for young adult female actors (Scirocco Drama). Her award-winning play *SHIKSA* premiered with the Jewish Theatre in 2016.

Of late, Cairn has been busy resurrecting ghosts from our history books in her new play *Shinny*—a story of the brave and determined Canadian women who fought a 125-year battle to play professional hockey. Each spring, Cairn heads to her lake house in a little beach town called Gimli, where she spends her time writing, Sea-Dooing, and directing a show at the charming A-Spire Theatre.